Uncensored

Sentenced to an Adult Maximum-Security Prison at Age 15

Uncensored

Sentenced to an Adult Maximum-Security Prison at Age 15

William H. Graves Jr.

Copyright

Printed in the United States of America.
First Printing, 2018

ISBN-13: 978-1-947656-45-1
ISBN10: 1947656457

The Butterfly Typeface Publishing
PO BOX 56193
Little Rock Arkansas 72215

Dedication

I dedicate this book to all the convicts (past and present) from 1968 until now who are in the Arkansas prison system; those that survived the hell hole as I did, and those who did not make it.

I also dedicate this book to all the people who are helping me to finish books 2 and 3 by questioning me about the inside of the prison and sharing my memories.

Foreword

This book and the others that will come after it, are the complete and uncensored truth about Arkansas Prisons and the prison system in general from 1968 to 2014 by an ex-convict who was there.

In writing these books, it is my intention to do all that I can to give you, the reader, a vivid and full understanding of the environment that I endured off and on from 1968 until 2014.

I also want you to comprehend the physical structure and environment of the prison in the 60's, 70's, 80's, 90's, and the new millennium.

Acknowledgments

I want to first give Thanks and Praise to our Lord and Savior Jesus Christ for allowing me o come out of my prison experience with my sanity, my manhood, and my goodness as a human.

Next, I want to give special thanks to Norma Jean Johnson for her assistance, for pushing me, for introducing me to the USB drive, and helping me to type. I couldn't have done it without her.

I also thank my nice for pushing me to do this even when I was in prison. Shirly Presley really stayed on me until I finished.

Finally, I want to give thanks to Sonta Jean, The KOKY Queen, for introducing me to my publisher, Iris M. Williams of Butterfly Typeface Publishing who has helped me present this masterpiece to you.

Love you all! Books 2 and 3 will be ready soon!

William H. Graves

AKA Uncle Willie

Table of Contents

Introduction

Tucker and Cummins were like no other prisons in the United States with possibly the exception of Texas, Alabama, and Mississippi. In my opinion, Cummins and Tucker were worse than all of them. The overall living conditions from 1968 until the 1990s were deplorable, barbaric, and inhumane. It was also lawless, where only the strong survived. For three decades inmates in the Arkansas Prison System never went to sleep comfortably and prayed that they would wake up for breakfast.

Inmates never went to work in the fields knowing that they would be safe and alive to finish the workday. Our lives hung in the balance day and night. This was an environment that was run by convict trustees and was supported by a handful of prison guards. I say convict trustees, but I really mean inmate trustees; convicts wouldn't have a job like this. (I will tell you more about the difference between an inmate and convict later.)

Now, let me relive my Journey and tell you my story.

When I arrived at Cummins prison in 1968, I was 15-years-old. At that time, the prison was segregated. East Hall was the living area for blacks and West Hall was the living place for whites. There were four barracks for each hall. One through four was West Hall, and five through eight was East Hall. Each barrack on East Hall had over 175 inmates confined in them. The barracks were built to hold only 80 men.

I was housed in barracks 5, (throughout the rest of this book) and there were over 183 inmates living in this barrack. The bunks were doubled (stacked on top of each other). There were only three long urinals and six toilets for all of these inmates. There were only 12 shower heads for over 175 inmates/convicts to shower under.

There were two TVs, one in front of the barracks and one in the back of the barracks; both were anchored to the bars. There were only 12 to 16 chairs in both areas for 175 guys to watch TV and 32 chairs for 175 inmates to sit. The rest of the men who wanted to watch TV either had to stand up or sit on the floor. This was the physical description for how all 4 barracks were on East Hall in 1968.

The barracks 4 on West Hall had the same physical structure as the East Hall, but there were fewer whites were in prison during the 60's and 70's. There might have been 100 or fewer whites in the West Hall barracks.

In 1969, the Cummins unit was integrated. The 1st barrack integrated was barracks 4. All the whites were moved out and barracks 4 was made into an integrated disciplinary barracks that housed the most incorrigible, belligerent inmates/convicts in the prison system (Cummins/Tucker). The administration put about 60 or 70 of us in this barrack. The other seven barracks remained segregated until 1970 when all barracks were integrated.

There was one barber chair that sat in the front of the barracks and one coffee pot. This was the physical structure of all 8 barracks. Then, barrack 4 was changed because it was converted into a punishment barrack, and it was stripped down.

The coffee pot, barber chair and everything else was moved out except the bunk beds. This is basically how all 8 barracks were set up. The difference at that time was that the West Hall barracks were less crowded because the population of whites was far less than the population of blacks.

Racism in the Jim Crow era was not only a factor for free men and women, it was also something convicts and inmates dealt with as well.

I should have never been sent to an adult prison because I was basically a child, and my crimes were not so heinous or atrocious that I had to be housed with hardened, seasoned, veteran convicts and inmates.

The barracks on West Hall reflected the Jim Crow Era in the justice of blacks being imprisoned while whites received a slap on the hand. The segregation period was truly reflected in the prison. There were big dining halls, and a big wall that went straight down the middle of it which separated whites from the blacks. So, the dining room was segregated, and we even worked in the fields separately.

The kitchen and dining hall were segregated also. Blacks ate on the East Hall side of the dining hall, and whites ate on the West Hall side.

The only things that were integrated at that time was the sick call procedure and yard.

In 1969, barrack 4, the disciplinary barrack, was the first barracks to eat in the dining hall as an integrated barrack. I was sixteen-years-old.

Ready For Prison

In October 1968, at the age of 15, I was sentenced to 18 months in the Arkansas Department of Corrections (A.D.C.) for the crime of forgery and uttering (spending counterfeit money).

While being sentenced to prison, it never crossed my mind nor my mother's mind that I was too young to be sentenced to an adult prison. We never realized that my crime wasn't that heinous or atrocious. However, I was sentenced to prison and not a Boy's Industrial School.

What did cross *my* mind was the fact that I kept telling myself I was ready for prison. I was not going to be scared or intimidated by being in prison. I was saying all of this because I had been to the Boy's Industrial School in 1966 and 1967. I was trying to psych myself out, so I wouldn't be afraid of going to prison.

When I arrived at Cummins, in October 1968, I, along with eight other guys, was placed on a wall to wait for processing into prison and for our assigned living area. While waiting on the wall, my eyes kept rolling around everywhere because I wanted to be aware of my surroundings.

Not even the Boy's Industrial School made me ready for what my eyes were witnessing. I remember saying to myself that I had never in my life seen so many weird looking people at one time.

Remember, I was only 15.

I was scared and intimidated a little bit, but not as badly as I wished I had been. I was kind of calm. I was curious about prison and sort of mesmerized to be in such an environment at the age of 15.

It was meal time when I arrived at Cummins, so I had a chance to see many faces and I remember being overwhelmed at what I was seeing. All I saw was a sea of black faces, and most of them had mean and vicious looks which scared me a little bit. I was doing my best to find at least one familiar face.

I was assigned to barracks 5. That first night at Cummins was an experience that I will never forget. It was dramatic to say the least.

There was a lot to see that first night.

A poker game was going on in the back of the barracks, as well as two dice games. There was green money being used and brozane (prison money) being used as well. They were drinking bootleg alcohol and Free World Bonded Whiskey.

I walked by this one particular bed (remember all beds are stacked bunks) and there were make-shift curtains hanging from the top bunk. The curtains were actually sheets and blankets hanging around the bed forming a box tent.

With this being my first introduction to prison life and me not knowing any better, I allowed my curiosity to compel me to peep inside the tent through the exposed area. I was totally flabbergasted and amazed by what I saw.

There were two men in bed naked. One of the men was on the other man's back grinding, and all I could think to say was, "Damn."

I did have enough sense to walk on, and I believe that move saved my life.

After the big black dude (the one on top) finished his business, he came up to the area where I was standing and started talking to me while I stood there with my two homeboys and rap (crime) partner.

He said, "Young ass nigga, don't you ever do shit like that again. If you care anything about your life, you won't ever make that mistake again. Because if you do, I will take your life or your manhood, and I don't care which one I get from you. You understand?"

Before I could say anything, one of my homeboys spoke up and said, "We got you on that, Crow. This is his first day in the joint, and he really didn't know any better, but he does now. It won't happen again."

Crow said, "It better not." Then, as he walked away he said, "If it does, you'll be in the tent next."

I was about to say something back when all three of my homeboys said, "Shut up! That nigga will kill you and all of us too!"

So, I left it alone.

That was my introduction to prison life in the Arkansas Department of Corrections at the age of 15.

The Prison Officers

The next day I had to go to work in the Long Line.

The Long Line was one big squad of about 120 to 150 workers. We were guarded by other inmates that were called Trustees. They carried shotguns and 30.06 rifles. Each one had a pistol strapped to his side, it was usually a 38 or 44.

My rider was an Inmate Trustee who was over everybody. His title was Long Line Rider. He carried a stick and rode on horseback, back and forth down the line behind the workers checking on their work.

There were also Inmate Generals who worked under the Rider. It was their job to catch whatever the Rider missed. The Generals and the Riders were also usually sexual predators on the lookout for any weak, scared individual whom they could prey upon for sexual favors and release. They would also use them for financial gain.

Most of the Generals were guys who had been victimized themselves and had given up their manhood. To keep them from being a problem, the Riders allowed them to portray the role of a female; performing sexual acts, cooking, and making the beds of their protector.

The Rider allowed those two or three to become Generals or just to step out of the line. That was where I was trying to fit in. All you had to do was show that you didn't mind killing or maiming anyone who crossed your path wrong. I just wasn't ready to deal with Crow after the night that he intimidated me. Plus, I might just have been daydreaming, or fantasizing in my young mind about becoming one of the Generals.

In 1968 and 1969, there was no one to take your problems and concerns to except another inmate. But that could get you killed because the inmate whom you complained to or cried to was probably going to tell the next inmate you had complained about; the one you talked about was going to have you beaten by other inmates working in the field because you wanted a couple of days off from work. So, they beat you badly enough to lay you up in the Infirmary.

There was only one officer who often was on two, 12-hour shifts watching over 700 or 800 men. So sometimes they used us to help them.

This one Free World Officer picked out about six so-called tough inmates to help him run his shift. He rewarded them by allowing them to go all over the prison. He brought them Free World Liquor, marijuana, and acid to make money. He also allowed them to pursue any young victim they desired to have sexual relations with. He just made them promise that they would not rape and kill anyone. Plain rape was alright, but not killings.

There are defining differences between an inmate and a convict. And it was those differences that determined a man's role in prison.

An inmate is basically an ass-kisser and snitch, as well as, a semi-weak individual. Some inmates are fighters too who are skilled in keeping an adversary off their ass. Most inmates work for The Administration and are the Captain's, Major's, and Asst. Warden's eyes and ears.

A convict is a person who does his own time, minds his own business, and is dangerous. A convict is also a leader and an adversary to The Administration. He's proficient at writing grievances, lawsuits, and letters of complaints. He's admired and looked up to by the other inmates and convicts. He is disliked but respected by security officers, ranking officers, and The Administration, but they refuse to trust working him in a high-security area that gives access to vital information which could harm the prison or that unit.

A convict is also a person who refuses to remain complacent or subservient about bad policies and bad situations. A convict refuses to ignore or to stay silent about discrimination of himself and others and refuses to ignore any abuse of others.

Convicts are guys like George Jackson (you older people will know him) of the Soledad Brothers and Tookie Williams (the younger people will recognize him) who was executed because he wouldn't kiss ass with the Governor of California.

There are a few other convicts that could or would add a little more to the distinct difference between the two terms, but not by much.

There were four officers total on East Hall, two for day shift and two for night shift. When one officer was off, the other one was on. There were four on West Hall (the white end of prison), with the same work schedule.

There was a Major, Assist. Warden, and Warden also, but we very seldom saw any of them. The

Trustee Inmates who wore khaki uniforms ran the prison. The Warden and Assist Warden only set policy for the prison to be run by the Inmates Trustees, and they were to enforce the policies and regulations.

In 1968 and 1969, it was a system where only the strong survived, and snitching was a no-no and/or taboo because that got you killed during this era. No one really snitched because there were no secrets.

There were Floorwalkers assigned to seven of the eight barracks (barracks 8 was the Trustee's barracks, and there were three inmates assigned to keep it clean).

There were six Floorwalkers assigned to each barracks; three on the day shift and three on the night shift. These Floorwalkers were responsible for keeping the order inside the barracks for the officers. They were his eyes and ears; they put out physical discipline to the unimportant guys who got beside themselves and stole from the wrong people or became too noisy.

The Floorwalkers were usually big, heavy-set, solidly built guys, and some were very muscular type dudes, but all 6 of them would be tough and dedicated to doing their job as a Floorwalker. They would be totally dedicated to the Free World Officers, and none of us challenged the Floorwalkers unless we were ready to kill. So, we just never challenged their authority.

There were also Trustee Guards on the picket at the back of the barracks. A picket is an area where jail cell bars separated the trustee from the barracks and the inhabitants of the barracks. The purpose of the picket is to hold clothes and for the shotgun guard to hold the post and guard the barracks. The guards on the picket were also there to provide adequate backup to the Floorwalkers.

Those guards carried double barrel shotguns, and they never hesitated to use them. They were loaded with a birdshot, and sometimes they were loaded with salt or other material that was meant to wound or disable you.

A Big Argument

In 1967, at Tucker Unit, a big argument started in barracks 2 about the television.

This big white Floorwalker (6'3" 240 lbs.) named Larry Hudson changed the channel on the T.V. and walked back to his bed.

We were watching Soul Train. He put the T.V. on some junk station that he wanted to watch. I got up, put the T. V. back on Soul Train, and stood there for a moment.

When I saw Floorwalker Hudson coming back to change the T.V. I asked, "Why are you messing with the T.V. on this side when there is a big T.V. on the other side?"

"Because I'm the fucking Floorwalker," he replied. "And I can change the T.V. whenever I want to. You and no one else, unless you're a Floorwalker, better not touch the fucking T.V. again or I will kick your little black ass."

I was really amazed that he would say this to me because there were at least fifteen other blacks and about four whites who were also watching Soul Train; and at least three of the people watching were as big as Floorwalker Hudson.

They were mad about dude changing the T.V. channel too. So, when Floorwalker Hudson changed the T.V. back to his station, I changed it back to Soul Train, and then immediately threw a punch that hit the Floorwalker in the face with all the power I had.

All the other people behind me immediately rushed the Floorwalker and began beating him. When the other two Floorwalkers came to help him, they were beaten down as well because we had numbers and were ready to fight.

A lot of guys got out of bed to help us beat these Floorwalkers down. We then heard a loud noise that sounded like a firecracker or a gun.

That's when I heard some of my partners hollering, "Damn I just got shot!"

All of us started to disperse because the shotgun guard on the picket hollered, "Scatter!"

He had fired shots into the crowd that hit about eight or nine of us in the chest, back, leg, arm, feet, and hand. The shot was to give help and aid to the Floorwalkers being attacked. No one was hit in the face, and none of the guys who were hit had any serious injuries because the guard fired birdshots.

The inmate guard didn't kill anyone which really surprised all of us because there was an unwritten rule or policy in existence at that time.

Any Trustee Guard who was forced to kill any inmates in the line of duty would be given a 5-day furlough home.

When the Asst. Warden, Major, and shift officer came to the barracks to investigate what had happened, they immediately notified the Infirmary and sent the eight inmates who had got shot to be checked out as well as the Floorwalkers who had been beaten by all of us.

The Asst. Warden, Major, and another officer took some of us into the hallway and questioned us about the incident. When it became obvious that the Floorwalkers had started the fight, they issued a lot of threats to us about what they were going to do if anything like this happened again.

They told me I had better sit my young ass down somewhere and go on home before I get buried. This was supposed to be an intimidating threat to me, but I only laughed to myself because I had now established myself as a young tough guy.

I laughed to myself (to keep from being locked up"
and said, "Yes sir."

They didn't lock any of us, but they did transfer
Floorwalker Hudson, back to Cummins the next
day.

The Integration Process

I assumed that they didn't lock any of us up
because they had just integrated Tucker and the
Floorwalker had caused all the chaos and
mayhem.

Also, the N.A.A.C.P. and the A.C.L.U. had been
monitoring the integration process at both
Tucker and Cummins. They were watching for
discrimination towards blacks. They were also
watching and monitoring to see if any more
killings of inmates were going to occur and to see
if the prison system was going to try to continue
to use the strap to whip the inmates with.

So, The Administration wasn't too eager to attract any unwanted attention to the prison system. The Commissioner (called The Director here in modern day time), at the time, was Mr. H. Jerome Harper who was sort of a Politician.

Harper ran the Arkansas Prison System and was appointed by the former governor, Winthrop Rockefeller. The Warden at Cummins was Mr. Ralph Roberts. The Warden at Tucker was Mr. Jack Finch who was also handpicked by Gov. Rockefeller to run Tucker because of how liberal minded he was.

Mr. Rockefeller wanted the negative aura surrounding Tucker to disappear and Mr. Finch was the man to do it.

Mr. Finch's wife, Mrs. Harriet Finch, was hired to establish and run an educational program because the Federal Government wanted education to be available to the inmates at Tucker.

The Assistant Warden at Cummins was Mr. Cee Bee Loren (later killed in 2003 by an escaped convict).

The Assistant Warden at Tucker was Mr. William Barker.

The sole purpose of me telling you who the Wardens and Assistant Wardens were from 1968 to 1970 is to authenticate all the other facts in my books and to show you how sharp my memory is on recalling the facts about the entire prison system. Most of the information I'm sharing with you can be verified and the small percentage that can't is either due to terrain changes or people being dead.

After the integration of barracks 4 in 1969 at Cummins, I was one of the first young convicts to be assigned there. Barracks 4 was the first barracks to be integrated at Cummins. (Later in my story I'll explain this integration in greater detail including all the atrocities and mayhem that occurred to the inmates there.)

How I got placed in Barracks 4

I was confined at the Tucker Unit in 1969 and was working on the Long Line.

One day a black inmate name Brunston Gregory got into a fight in the field (the field was outside where crops were grown) with a white inmate, and the Long Line Rider (Tucker hired Free World Field Riders at this time) shot his pistol in the air a few times to break up the fight.

The white inmate had started the fight by calling Brunston a nigger, spook, jigaboo, and other derogatory names. The rider never told the white inmate to shut up although he heard everything that the white inmate said to Brunston.

Brunton said, "I'm tired of your mouth, and I'm going to beat your ass when we get in so, I won't have to worry about getting shot when we get in."

The white inmate immediately attacked Brunston although he knew he couldn't whoop Brunston because Brunston was much bigger than him. The white inmate would receive a brief, good ass whopping from attacking someone twice his size.

When the Rider finally broke the two men up, he had the two fighters step out of the work line, so he could talk to them. It was obvious that the Rider was racist because he jumped all over the Brunston verbally as if it were his fault.

We quit for lunch and went inside. When we arrived at the building, the Rider immediately took Brunston, locked him up in the hole (isolation), and let the white inmate go.

I immediately began to instigate a sit down (a work stoppage) because this was racism and discrimination, and I knew at the young age of 16 that if I let this slide, the Rider would get worse.

So, I convinced all the blacks working on the Long Lines and some of the whites to participate in the work stoppage. All of us refused to go back to work on the Long Line.

Mr. Barker, the Assistant Warden, and some more Free World People came to the barracks to find out why we were refusing to go back to work.

I stepped to the front of the line and said, "Your Rider locked a black inmate up for fighting and let the white inmate go, and the white inmate started the fight by calling the black inmate all kind of niggers, jigaboos, and anything else he could think of to call the black inmate. The Rider heard all of this but chose to lock up the black inmate for defending himself. None of us are going back to work until the black inmate is released from Isolation, or we talk to Warden Finch."

Mr. Barker said something I can't recall and departed the area. About 2 hours later, they released Brunston from Isolation.

The next morning around 9 am, Mr. Barker sent for Brunston Gregory, William Furr, Otis Taylor, Spanky Stewart, Donald Adams, and me.

When we arrived up front, we were seated on benches with our backs to them in the lobby. The Assistant Warden, Mr. Barker, the Major, and someone else came out to talk to us.

They began telling us that there wasn't any prejudice, that their goals were to make sure this integration worked, and that blacks were treated as equal to the whites.

Everything being said sounded really good to us. I was especially impressed until the Assistant Warden said, "My best friend as a young man was a black guy, so I am definitely not prejudiced."

I was 16-years-old, at the time, but I had heard this declaration by whites numerous times and I always tried to respond in the same manner.

"Mr. Barker," I said. "If you are so solid and you aren't prejudiced, then will you answer this question for me?"

"Sure, Willie."

"If you came home one night, walked into the living room, and discovered me, at the age of 16, having sex with your 18-year-old daughter, how would you react since I am black?"

His entire face turned beet red. I could see the anger and surprise visible in his face, and he couldn't give me a response.

"You don't have to answer, Mr. Barker," I continued. "Your face has already supplied the answer, and you should resign your position because you are definitely prejudiced because there is no way you can look at me and see a fellow human being with just different skin pigmentation."

"Go pack all of their property and bring it back," Mr. Barker told his Major. "Put all of them on the van along with their property."

"Mr. Barker," I said. "Did my question anger you so much that you are fixing to kill all of us and bury us with our property?"

"No Willie," he said. "I am sending you back to Cummins because I believe that you are older than 16, and I don't need you here trying to run my Penitentiary. I run this prison not Willie, *goddamn Graves the 16-year-old*, and since you don't know this and you've conveniently forgotten this, I'm sending you somewhere where they are equipped to deal with you better than we are."

And with that, all of us were loaded onto the van and transferred to Cummins.

Arriving at Cummins

The things I am writing about are true and not exaggerated. These are factual incidents of what happened to me and the other guys. I know they seem unreal because they are so deplorable, but it is true and even at the young age of 15, I knew that the prison system was flawed and needed work in order to perfect it.

When I arrived at Cummins, I was immediately placed in the disciplinary barracks which was barracks 4. Although it was the only integrated barracks at Cummins, Barracks 4 was set up to house the most incorrigible, belligerent, and hardcore prisoners in the system at that time. How do you classify hardcore and belligerent prisoners within the A.D.C.?

I hadn't been in prison a total of six months yet, and already classified as such. That's the way it was done during this era. I was placed in the discipline barracks; the very first administrative segregated barracks ever established in the history of A.D.C.

This barracks was established to teach any and every convict assigned to it that they weren't as tough as they thought they were.

They wanted us to know that we could be treated anyway that the state wanted to treat us, and we couldn't do anything about it.

The inmates assigned to live in this punishment barrack knew this and were being cautious and checking each other out because this was the most dangerous barrack in the entire prison system. No one wanted to make a mistake and get killed in the process.

We all knew that we were put there to hopefully start killing each other off or at least to hurt each other enough so that we couldn't be considered a threat to the prison system in any way anymore.

As convicts, we wanted to see who was weak, who was a problem, who was a snitch, and who could end up being a sissie for the barracks. We also wanted to establish who was going to be the leader without voting him the leader.

After three days had passed, we settled in.

We went to work again and Mr. G.W. Smith AKA *Big Snasty* had his two Riders (inmates McAllen and Beatty) to really work us like we were real slaves. The Riders were talking badly to us. They were calling us sorry S.O.B.s, dick-eating motherfuckers, and other derogatory names. They were doing this just for the hell of it and to make matters worse, they didn't give us our water breaks.

Finally fed up, I threw my hoe up in the air and said, "I quit if I can't get any water."

One of the riders got off his horse and gave his gun to another Rider.

He walked up to me and said, "Young ass nigga, you better grab that hoe and get your ass back to work, or I'm going to kick your ass all over this turn row (the end or the start of the field) and then you are still going to work."

"You can start kicking," I replied. "Because I'm through working because you aren't going to treat me like no damn slave, and you damn sure aren't going to work me like no slave or inhuman person. Not you, your boss, or co-workers."

By this time about fifteen more convicts had thrown their hoes in the air. Some of them landed close to the Rider making him realize that he needed to move his ass away from our area.

All of us quit and the Rider marched all of us to the airplane strip. Their plan was to keep all of us out there on the strip until dark. This is what was done.

The temperature was about 101 degrees and the mosquitoes and gnats were present like a swarm over us. It was so hot that we could hardly breathe because we were made to sit on the ground. The ground was as hot as an oven and as it started to get dark, the mosquitoes started to bite and hum all around our heads. Some of us began to use our hands to dig trenches or holes to get in and covered ourselves up with the dirt. We pulled our shirts over our heads to keep the mosquitoes off of our faces and necks while the dirt protected our lower bodies.

After it got dark, they gathered all of us together, loaded us on a flatbed truck, and took us to the prison compound. But instead of taking us in into the building to our barracks, we were taken to the softball field. All of us were made to spend the night on the softball field battling the outdoor heat as well as the mosquitoes. We were given water and a bologna sandwich around midnight.

The next morning, we were lined up and marched to the barracks. We were allowed to shower and change clothes; then, we were escorted to the kitchen to eat breakfast. After breakfast, we were taken back to our barracks. We got three to four hours of sleep, before being were called for chow. During that time the Rider made a speech basically telling us we could go through the same procedure or we could go back to work.

He said, "It's left entirely up to you."

I stood up and said, "I'm not going to work, and I'm not going to the airstrip or softball field anymore. You guys created all this bullshit, and I'm not about to let you treat me like no slave. When you learn how to give me proper water breaks and how to quit trying to run me, then I will gladly come to work." I sat down and finished eating.

Upon exiting the kitchen, Beatty said, "Young blood, if you go to work, I promise you that everyone will get their proper water breaks and we won't run you or cuss you guys no more."

I felt that he was telling the truth, so I went back to work.

McAllen's Stupidity

One month later, McAllen began talking about certain guys' families and continued calling them derogatory names like sorry ass, dick suckers, dick-eating bitches, and other bad names.

An inmate named Otis Reed told all of us to stay out of the way when McAllen came into the barracks at lunch time. No one asked why because we knew from the look on his face and the fact that he asked us to do something like that, that he was going to kill McAllen or try to anyway.

When McAllen came into the barracks to run his mouth, Otis Reed walked up to him and started sticking him with a big long knife that looked like a sword.

Otis stuck McAllen in the back, chest, arms, and stomach. In the struggle, McAllen almost overpowered Otis Reed and took the knife from him. That's when another guy, named Robert Courtney, came to Reed's aid and helped him by putting McAllen in a chokehold from behind.

Reed proceeded to kill McAllen by continuously sticking him. He stuck McAllen at least 20 to 30 times.

McAllen's refusal to run out the door when he was first struck with the knife is what led to his demise. McAllen wanted to try to fight. So it was his stupidity that got him killed.

Otis Reed

Otis Reed was locked up in Isolation for 3 weeks. Then, he was placed back in the barracks because, during the 60s and 70s, prisoners were rarely taken to court and persecuted for killing another inmate.

For example, a guy named Royce Murphy stabbed and killed Hershel Atkinson (a black inmate) at Tucker in 1969 for calling him a one-eyed, ugly ass, white dog. Royce received the death sentence (later converted to life without by Governor Rockefeller).

We never totally understood this because Murphy had killed another inmate by stabbing him to death over a poker game. So there was no way that he should have been let off of death row.

That is the way that we felt at that time because to the black inmates, we felt that this was an act of racism. We felt that his fate should have been sealed when he killed Hershel.

Tucker Prison had just integrated in 1968 and the blacks felt that Royce should get either life without parole or the death penalty, but that's just how it was in 1968, 1969 and 1970. The guys incarcerated in prison were simply in another world, *The Twilight Zone.*

Guys never did any more than three to four weeks in Isolation for killing another inmate. That's just how it was then. No one was really punished for killing fellow inmates.

One week after Otis Reed was released from Isolation, one of my best friends, named Spanky Stewart got into it with a guy named Calvin Paschal who was a total and complete bully.

Paschal was bullying Spanky for some reason, and Spanky was scared as hell.

What got me involved was when Paschal hit Spanky with a pair of knee high, rubber boots and said, "Now, go tell your man Willie Graves about what I did to your weak ass, and both of you can come see me." He laughed and walked to his bed.

Calvin Paschal was built like Tony Atlas or The Rock. I was 16, but fairly nicely built myself. So, I went to Paschal and asked him why he pulled me into his fucked-up bullshit.

He replied, "Because you are supposed to be some kind of Godfather to these other dudes, but you aren't shit to me."

I responded, "I don't want to be shit to you, but I'm the wrong motherfucker to have as an enemy. So, you need to slow your roll with me bro, and if you want me involved, you have just succeeded in involving me because I'm part of this show now. And you know that Spanky nor I involve ourselves in that gay, homosexual stuff. I don't believe you truly wanted me involved in none of this. I think you were bumping your gums and now you realize that you have bit off more than you can chew."

I walked away, and he said nothing. Our discussion only lasted about ten minutes and I was glad he reacted like a true bully because I had no idea if I could whip him or not. But, I do know that if I hadn't confronted him or if I had confronted him in a passive manner, he would have done me worse than he did to Spanky.

Killing Paschal

Paschal knew that Spanky was my best friend since we were in the reform school together, and what he did and said was totally disrespectful to Spanky and me. So, I made up my mind to go ahead and kill him.

That night while Paschal was asleep in his bed, I got up and went to obtain a 10-inch knife from a close friend. All he had was an 8-inch blade with about 2 inches of wooden handle. The blade was razor sharp. About a ½ inch on both sides of the blade had a stiletto-like point on it.

The rest of the blade point was kind of serrated so that after you stuck a person and pulled the blade out, some of their guts came out too.

That was my weapon to be used to kill this germ.

I talked big, but when it was on my mind about killing a dude, I was scared to death.

Again, I was only 16 and this was my first decision to kill anyone.

I went to the bathroom and there where an old bed on the floor of the bathroom (it was torn up and waiting to be fixed or thrown away). I got on my knees and said a simple prayer. I remember this prayer like it was yesterday.

"Lord, this isn't your conventional everyday prayer, and I apologize, but I'm fixing to kill this ignorant ass nigga unless you send me an omen to spare his life. If you send an officer down the hall in the next 15 to 20 seconds, THEN I KNOW YOU WANT HIM TO LIVE. If you don't want him to live, then I will end his life and add him to satan's list because I'll know you don't want him."

I got up and began to walk around the barracks looking at my watch every 25 seconds. I went and got the knife. It was my intention to stab him in the heart, but as scared as I was, I felt I might miss his heart because of how much my hand was shaking. So, I made up my mind to hit him in the goosier pipe (the throat).

I stabbed down to hit him dead in the throat because I knew that if I hit him right, he wouldn't live. But instead, I hit him on the side of his goosier pipe and only nicked a micro of an inch of his goosier pipe.

He lived.

When they took him to the hospital, they never questioned me or anything, but they still locked me up and released me three days later.

Two days afterward, they released Calvin Paschal from the Infirmary and put him in barracks 4, the same barracks he was originally in with me.

I walked past him immediately, so he would fully realize and know that I wasn't scared of him. If he did anything wrong again, I wouldn't miss him next time. I would kill him.

Paschal could barely talk and he muttered, "Let me talk to you."

"What you want?"

"Man, I don't know if you got me or not, but I don't want no more trouble."

"Yeah, it's ok," I said. "And I'll be watching your ass."

Two weeks later, Calvin was transferred to Tucker.

Somewhere towards winter, Mr. Cee Bee Loren called me into his office and told me that due to my age, he was releasing me from the disciplinary barracks.

Mr. Loren was the Asst. Warden, and he was hard as hell. He was short and kind of dumpy with glasses. We called him names like Humpty Dumpty. The inmates felt that he had a complex about his physical build which was why he allowed the mistreatment of us by the Riders. His Riders used to force inmates to stand on top of milk crates in the field as punishment for small violations.

Mr. Loren carried a slapjack in his hand at all times and he would help his building (Major Purtle, then Major Fletcher) whip inmates in the confinement of the Major's office.

This was a big deal back then because we all dreaded being called to the Major's office because there was a 7 out of 10 chance that we were going to be beaten and locked up in Isolation until the swelling went down.

Another Sit Down

Around October of 1969 I instigated another sit-down for all of Cummins.

I did it because the Federal Courts had ruled the Arkansas Department of Corrections (A.D.C.) unconstitutional. The inmates were being abused in that the Trustees were being allowed to drag inmates out of the barracks and whip them with nightsticks, slapjacks, and throw us in the hole.

The hole was a cell with no bunks or beds. It had a combined commode and a sink made of concrete. The cells were only big enough to house two people, but at all times, there were at least four to six inmates in a cell.

We were at work in a soybean field when all of us quit work. I had preached to all of the inmates that the only way to make our incarceration time better was to show society how ill and sick-minded these folks were in regards to how they treated us (feedings while in the hole, allowing other inmates to decide our daily fate and existence, and poor sleeping conditions the in barracks).

If I rolled over, I would be in my neighbor's bed!

When we went to work the next day, we threw our hoes up in the air and quit. Immediately, all the Farm Managers, Farm Supervisors, the Assist Warden, Cee Bee Loren, and every Free World male personnel available came and grabbed nightsticks, shotguns, and rifles and surrounded both Long Lines.

A speech was made by Cee Bee Loren giving us a chance to leave the sit-down. Over half the inmates chose to leave the sit-down. Then, they combined the lines together.

Mr. Dolphous, a skinny white dude who was a Farm Supervisor, started walking towards me with the intentions of hitting me with his nightstick. I went low, dumped him on the ground, and hurriedly backed up. If I had got straddled by him, I would have been immediately shot and possibly killed.

So, when I jumped back, I hollered to Mr. Loren and said, "I am not going to allow any of you to bust my head with no nightstick or to even hit me with one. This is a peaceful sit-down work stoppage. It is not a riot. We aren't preaching any violence."

Mr. Loren spoke out again, "I am going to give anyone the chance to leave this area that wants to go. Anyone that doesn't leave is going to the hole, and this will be their permanent resident as long as I'm Asst. Warden."

Everybody left but 25 guys.

All of us were taken behind the levee, and Cee Bee Loren, Victor Day, and three or four other supervisors and Free World Long Line Riders were with them. They told us that they were considering burying us behind this levee in order to be done with a pain in the ass problem from a handful of damn fools.

He then said, "But I can't chance going to prison for multiple murders, so I'm going to take all of you to the hole and let you spend some time in my private motel."

The 1983 Lawsuit

We were housed four convicts to a cell.

One dude was cut loose because he was a little mentally challenged. The Asst. Warden called and ordered him to be released.

We were packed in the cell like sardines. The commodes in the cells were like old outdoor shit houses. They didn't flush. We had to keep a top over it at all times.

Our living conditions were inhumane and totally indecent.

I kept asking for some writ paper (typing paper) and the officers kept refusing me. So, I got a roll of toilet tissue and began to file my 1983 lawsuit on toilet tissue. I used over 100 sheets, mailed it out, and the court accepted it.

The Honorable J. Smith Henley accepted my lawsuit.

The lawsuit Willie Graves vs. Jerome Harper was written and filed in 1969. It was the first time in the history of the State of Arkansas that an inmate had filed a lawsuit in Federal Court on toilet tissue.

The court accepted it because the first allegation was the State's refusal to pass out writ paper.

One of the ways the lawsuit was resolved was that the court required Cummins, Tucker, and 4Camp (the women's unit that was a block down from

Cummins) to always have a record of passing out writ paper with the inmate's signature to verify that he had received writ paper.

This was called the Willie Graves Rule for years by the officers who desired to be sarcastic.

While I was locked up in the hole, two of the guys locked up with me were put in the cell with a special needs inmate named Gerald Biddle, a white inmate who was partially mentally challenged.

The two guys put in the cell with him were Ira Wallace AKA Um-Gawa and Presley Hill. Both of them were black and were a little challenged themselves.

I can't elaborate a whole lot on the subject because I wasn't in the cell with them, but I was four cells down from them and heard what was going on. Plus, Presley Hill and Ira Wallace was communicating with us while they were raping Gerald.

When Gerald began to fight back, both Presley and Ira conspired to kill him.

Since no one else was in the cell with them, they had to know that they were going to have a rape and a murder charge, but they were too dumb to care until Biddle's body was discovered a day later.

The officers only made security checks when they felt like it and then only glanced inside the cells.

Both Wallace and Hill ended up getting long sentences. Prior to the rape, their original sentences were short (only five or ten years at the most).

Wallace is dead, and Hill is currently at Tucker.

Home

In December of 1969, I was released from the hole, and a few weeks before Christmas, I went home. I was 17-years-old.

I was a kid at the age of 15 when I went to prison in October 1968. I had two birthdays while I was there.

Influenced by the environment I was in, I was forced into to becoming a man.

If I had allowed myself to remain a child when I was incarcerated, I would have become a sissy wearing panties, mascara, and halter tops. That's what happened to a lot of young people who went to prison and refused to grow up.

I personally saw numerous young guys get turned into sissies.

Hogan Green was in the reform school in 1966 and 1967. Although he was only 15 or 16 himself, he was personally turning 12, 13, and 14-year-olds into sissies. He was a predator. He was tough, and he could fight.

But when I got to prison in 1968, I saw Hogan Green portraying the role of a female. He was being kissed by his prison protector whom also was fondling and caressing his buttocks.

My point is that just because a person claims to be tough and hardcore does not automatically make it so. The younger a person is when they go to prison, the greater the chances are that they are going to be a victim of some form of a sexual relationship with a much older inmate.

I came to prison at a young age, but I refused to be anything but a man child. I was 15 and the fact still remains that I was a child in an adult world full of murderers, rapists, child molesters, robbers, and drug dealers. I still refused to be a victim in prison in any way. Even though I was young, I made up my mind that I was not going to be a sissy in prison.

In December of 1969, I was released from prison because I had flattened my 18 months sentence and free to go home. Going free was a joy but was also sad because I had lost my mother.

Anger and Injustices

I was 16 when my mother was robbed and murdered. The perpetrator was never caught. My little sisters and two brothers were now living in Texas with relatives. I was totally down on life at this point. I took it personally that my mother had been robbed and murdered.

The police didn't even arrest a possible suspect or bring anyone in for questioning. So, I took that as a personal affront, and decided to stay in my small life of crime. I was mad and hurt, so I kept committing crimes. I was sent back to prison at the age of 17 for attempted burglary. I was given 30 months for throwing a brick through a jewelry store window with the *intentions* of ransacking the jewelry store and stealing all of the watches and chains in the store. However, the police got there before I could enter the premises. I was immediately arrested, taken to jail, and charged with attempted burglary. I was taken to court and sentenced to 30 months in prison. There is no doubt in my mind that I should never have been sent back to prison for something as frivolous as attempted burglary.

My mother (who was a single parent) realized prior to her death, that my being sent to prison three times in three years (at the age of 15 in 1968 for forgery and uttering, for a parole violation in 1969 [after being released that same year], and for attempted burglary in 1970) was primarily because I was a young black man with no connections to influential whites.

My prison time was also due to the fact that I was a young black male who had no idea how to focus attention on the *way* I was being treated.

No one could intervene and possibly get my convictions overturned because I was a child, and none of the crimes that I had committed were so serious or atrocious that I had to be sent to *prison* where there were adult murderers, rapists, drug dealers, and child molesters.

Yet, I was put in prison three times in two years for petty frivolous crimes.

The police did not do a formal investigation when my mother was murdered. In fact, I believed at the time that the police were mad at me because of my criminal activities at such a young age, so they chose not to pursue my mother's murderer. This only angered me to the point of wanting to harass the police.

No one wakes up and expects to do something that will send him to prison. However, I was angry and I wanted to commit crimes and beat the police by stealing, robbing, forging, and get away with it.

The police charged me with attempted burglary. I was convicted and sentenced to 30 months in prison. The sentencing judge was Henry Britt. He was the same judge that sentenced me to 18 months in prison back in 1968 for forgery and uttering.

The same day that Judge Britt sentenced me to prison at age 15, the judge and prosecuting attorney saw fit to remand a 16-year-old white guy back to juvenile jurisdiction. The 16-year-old white guy had been arrested and charged with simple robbery and burglary.

This particular incident shows the racial discrimination and racism that was going on in the late 60s. I understood that Judge Britt sentenced me to prison because I had been to a reform school twice, and the young white guy had never been in trouble.

Whatever the reason was for what Judge Britt did, the glaring fact still stands out that a young 15-year-old black kid went to prison for forgery and uttering, and a 16- year-old white kid was sent to The Boys Industrial School in Alexander, or he might have gotten probation.

However, his crimes were robbery and burglary.

Back to Cummins

When I arrived back to Cummins in 1970, I wasn't shocked by anything I saw.

I was re-entering a modern-day Sodom and Gomorrah. I also felt that I was now a veteran of prison life because this was my third trip to the big house. I was once again put in barracks 5 and on the Long Line.

Then, all the barracks were realigned, and all the Trustees were moved to the newly created barrack 9 which was outside and off to itself.

The Long Line workers were put in barracks 5.

In 1970, more officers had been hired to run the prison because the Federal Court had ruled the Arkansas Prison System unconstitutional and had ordered the A.D.C. to phase out the inmates guarding inmates and inmates supervising inmates.

All this accomplished was the guys started snitching on different people. It also started something with the officers; they started using their slapjacks and nightsticks.

The officers were also paying the guys in Hobby Craft to pad their slapjacks with extra lead. They (the Officers) were having anywhere from 2 to 6 lbs. of extra lead put in their slapjacks, and when they hit an inmate, the inmate was knocked out, or he had a good size knot on his head somewhere.

One day I had just gotten tired of seeing my close friends locked up and beaten because of those snitching ass cowards that thought they were doing some secret ass, good undercover snitching.

They thought that none of us knew who they were, but they were wrong. We knew who most of them were and had a general idea of their names.

So, the first thing that we did was shut the prison down by quitting work.

Nobody assigned to work in the fields was going to work. When they called work time, all three barracks, 5, 7, and 8 refused to go to work, and half of the inmates in barracks 6 also refused to go to work.

We then proceeded to carry out our plan and began to whip (beat) all of the known snitches out of the barracks.

This included the ones that we suspected were snitching. We didn't have the faintest idea that we were playing directly into Jerome Harper's hand.

The Commissioner, Mr. H. Jerome Harper, had called the Governor's Office and informed the Governor that he had a full-scale racial riot on his hands. He said he needed the State Troopers' assistance to break it up and to shut it down.

This was a complete and total lie by Mr. Harper. There was nothing racist about this work stoppage. Every inmate who was whipped out of the barrack received an *integrated* ass whipping by us.

Mr. Harper lied to the Governor's office and conned the Governor for his own personal reasons. Unfortunately, the Governor granted Mr. Harper's wish, and when the State Troopers arrived late in the night, the violent aspect of the situation was over.

All we were doing was sitting around waiting for an official to come talk to us. He wanted to see what it was that we wanted in order to go back to work. We never ever imagined that we would have to deal with the State Police in the manner that we did.

Just around 2:30 or 3:00 am, we saw the State Troopers outside taking over the Towers (this means taking over the outside guard stations that protect the security parameters of the unit) and lining up outside. It was funny to us, but I was laughing to cover up my fear because, in my mind, I saw abuse and misuse of us. It wasn't funny to me at all, but I wasn't in a position to show no fear because I was one of the three leaders who had got this sit-down started.

I was smart enough to know that no peaceful work stoppage or sit-down required State Police to come in and take over the outside of the prison.

I also knew that somehow what we were doing had been deemed more serious than what we were actually doing. The commissioner had lied.

So, I told all of my fellows that we were in for some really serious trouble and problems. When they asked me why I said that, I said, "I told you this because I have never heard of any prisons in the United States sending the State Police or National Guard into the prison to force the inmates to go to work, and it's a peaceful sit-down. So be prepared for anything."

Doing Their Job

Around 4:30 or 5:00 am, the State Police hit the hallways in a big group and were armed to the hilt. They threw the barrack's cell door open on barracks 12 and hollered, "Listen up, you maggots! You have exactly 45 seconds to get dressed and to get outside. Think I am joking if you want to but when I shut up, you will have only 15 seconds left. Then, I and my team will speed you up."

Once finished, he shut the door and moved to the side of the gate. I was the 5th or 6th person out because I wanted to see what they did to the first guys out. They did nothing, so I ran out myself.

The next thing I knew, I saw guys running out in their underwear and tee shirts only; some with one shoe on and one shoe off. Numerous guys ran out without being fully dressed, and it was cold as hell outside.

However, the State Police didn't care.

According to them, we had taken the penitentiary from Mr. Harper. They were there to take the prison back from us, to break us down, and to make sure the penitentiary would never be taken again because the inmates would know exactly what was coming. They were there to humble us and to make it known that we were criminals and that none of us were authoritative figures in any way. They wanted to show us that we were going to work and that we were going to work without any problems.

They made us do exercises, first. We did push ups, and whoever stopped before being told to was hit in the back of the neck or head with the butt of a carbine, rifle, or shotgun.

The State Police had us doing everything from sit-ups and toe touches to running in place, and push ups. Then, they went around trying to mess with us, to humiliate us in front of the other guys, to show them we weren't tough and we weren't running anything at all.

When they finally located me, I had my face buried in the ground trying to be as invisible as possible. They made me stand up and hit me in the stomach with the butt of a rifle.

When I went to my knees, they pulled me back up and said, "Willie Graves, from Hot Springs, the baby of the bunch, but also the so-called leader of this bullshit, hell, he isn't even 18 yet, but all of you are following this fucking baby."

They hit me in the stomach again and moved on to Ivory Holmes with Jessie Terry and some of the other leaders.

They worked all of us over, so when they felt that they had punished us enough, they gave everybody who wasn't fully dressed three minutes to get in the barracks, get fully dressed, and get back out there.

When the Commissioner and Warden tried to get involved, the State Police shoved them out of the way.

The State Police said, "You couldn't run your own damn prison, and let a bunch of inmates take it from you. You sent for us to get it back, so get the hell out of the way, and let us go to work and do our job."

K.K.K.

There was an incident where this white dude didn't have a shirt on, and he had K.K.K. tattooed on his back in big letters.

One of the black troopers saw it, stopped him, and asked the white inmate what K.K.K. meant. The white inmate didn't say anything, so about 4 or 5 Troopers asked him again what the letters stood for.

Then, the trooper said, "Don't answer, I'll figure it out myself." Shortly after, he said, "It stands for Kool Kolor Kids, doesn't it?"

The white inmate said, "Yes sir."

Two troopers hit him with their shotguns and said, "You are a damn lie."

They proceeded to rub it off with the stock of their carbines and rifles.

That's how hard it was for us on this day in 1970. The troopers were there to complete a mission; they wanted to break all of us and show us that we weren't as tough as we thought we were.

When everybody came back on the yard, they trotted us to the cotton fields. After running us through the cotton fields, they ran beside us, in front of us, and behind us. They gave us five minutes to catch our breaths. Then, they told us to get a cotton sack, catch a row, and go to work.

All of us did this except Arthur Rogers and Gilbert *Speck* Jackson. The troopers began beating Arthur Rogers first. The beating lasted three to five minutes before Arthur said he would go to work, and he did. *He's from Forrest City, and can and will verify this if he is still alive.*

They then started on *Speck* (Gilbert Jackson), and Speck had made up his mind that he wasn't going to work or pick even one boll of cotton. The State Troopers beat him. They dragged him to a row of cotton and did all that they could to break Speck. They beat his hands and feet; they did all of this so they could force him to pick just one boll of cotton.

They even told Speck that they would take him back in if he'd just pick one boll of cotton, but Speck spit in their faces and got another beating from the troopers.

Nevertheless, he never picked one boll of cotton.

The State Troopers left him lying in the mud and water at the end of the turn row. I believed his hands were broken. He was bleeding from the face, but he was never broken. He had shown all of us how much of a man he was and that he would stand for what he believed in even if he had to be tortured or even if he had to die.

All of us were mad at ourselves for submitting and we kinda wished that we could do it over again.

But then I said to myself, "I'm just glad that I'm still alive and healthy and that this ordeal with the troopers was over. I could move on. Youngster, you are 17 going on 35. No one expected you to do what Speck did, so quit tripping. None of us are the man Speck is."

The State Police had begun to leave, and the prison sent the Riders out as well as a truck to take Speck to the Infirmary. The Riders worked us about an hour just to make sure that they had everything under control. When they felt that they had everything under control, they loaded us up on the trailers and took us in.

I was still in semi shock about what had happened, but I kept my mouth shut on the ride to the building.

I heard a few of my friends saying to each other, "Damn man, them State Troopers did a job on Lil Willie, didn't they? I never thought I'd ever see the day when Lil Willie (me) was speechless on everything."

Things That Should Never Happen

I was messed up because the State Police had come in and literally destroyed all of us, the convicts and inmates. We had been beaten, humiliated, and practically brutalized.

A number of us realized that we couldn't have done anything but get maimed or killed, and there had been nothing, at all, that we could have done about it.

Gilbert *Speck* Jackson was the only man (convict) to stand up to them, and although his hands had been smashed and broken and he had really been beaten, he still never picked one boll of cotton.

The State Troopers left mad as hell at Speck because they failed to break him. On top of all this, I was still scared and couldn't disguise it.

I think it was the words of a State Trooper Sergeant that scared my young mind.

The Sergeant said, "Remember this you douchebags and scum. All of you are already paid for and if we kill anyone of you right now, it will be in the line of duty and we will only have eliminated a lot of scum from the face of the earth. So, please give us a good reason to start eliminating you and see if we'll hesitate to kill any one of you."

We were powerless to fight back or resist any of the intimidation tactics by the State Troopers. Anybody resisting or fighting back would have to be pain freaks that liked pain, and I definitely, did not like pain, in any manner.

If I could avoid it, I could avoid this by keeping my mouth shut.

So, yes, I was truly traumatized because the ordeal I had just gone through and witnessed. It was like something only seen in the movies.

This was not something that a young 18-year-old (this all happened in early December of 1970) was used to seeing in real life.

Guys beaten with carbines and tattoos erased off of a guy's body with the butts of a rifle leaving raw meat behind on the guy's back.

Guys' heads were smashed into the ground with the boots the troopers had on.

Arthur Rogers and Gilbert *Speck* Jackson were beaten by the State Police and Speck was literally beaten on just his knuckles until both hands were ruined for life and to the point of deformity.

These were things that never should have happened.

Blessed

I know that I should have felt blessed that I wasn't beaten worse than I was because I had been labeled as one of the leaders of the sit-down, but I didn't feel blessed.

I was traumatized to a degree, but I was also angry as hell because the Commissioner of Correction, Jerome Harper, had for some reason lied to the governor and told him a race riot had occurred in Cummins. He had flat out lied, and we could do nothing to expose him. Plus, all we wanted to do was get the news media, politicians, and Prison Rights Groups to see all of the inhumane, cruel and unusual punishments, and unconstitutional bullshit that was going on at Cummins.

We wanted to show everybody all of this and show them that nothing was going on inside the prison to eradicate any of it.

This was the sole purpose of our sit-down.

We wanted the media and outside agencies to get involved so that we could expose what was going on behind the prison gates, but Mr. Harper outflanked us and lied to the Governor about a fictional race riot.

It was a work stoppage because we had gotten tired of being abused by the Officers and Convict Trustees.

They were running us to and from work. They had formed goon squads that were jumping on various inmates. We were packed in the barracks like a can of sardines. We (the black inmates) were talked to the way the White Master and his overseer talked to slaves back in slavery days. We were tired of being treated like animals.

That was all of us. The whites and the blacks were tired. We all banned together for this work stoppage, and Mr. Harper knew this. He also knew that if we got the chance to talk to anyone, we would be able to expose all of the illegal, barbaric, and unconstitutional stuff that was going on. So, he lied to the governor and said he had a race riot on his hands.

When the State Troopers left, things did not immediately return to normal. The Officers and the Administration wanted to take advantage of the havoc and the fear that the State Troopers had instilled in everybody but Gilbert *Speck* Jackson. They wanted to pursue this ordeal to establish their dominance over us. Plus, they kept saying, if we have to bring them back, it's going to be twice as bad. They wanted to totally establish domination over the inmates and to keep us in awe and shock about what could be done to us if we ever decided to sit down again.

I started thinking that we were never in control of any part of the prison. Mr. Harper simply manipulated us and played us into starting this riot, so he could use the news media to help secure his job.

We were escorted in groups back to our own barracks. Then, we were fed one barracks at a time. The gun cage in the kitchen on both sides (East and West Hall) were manned by an Inmate Guard carrying a pump shotgun, and he stood where we could see him and his shotgun. After we were fed, the Major put two Inmate Trustee Guards and one Free World Officer on every barrack except the barracks outside; that was the Trustee Barrack.

The List

That night after the TVs went off and almost everybody was asleep, there was a goon squad consisting of four Inmates Trustees each with a nightstick piece along with 5 Free World Guards with nightsticks. They were authorized to go to every barrack and grab everybody whose name was on the list that the Warden and the Commissioner had put together.

This list was supposed to represent the leaders of the so-called racial riot and the names of the people who participated in the physical beatings of all known snitches and the suspected snitches.

The Administration wanted all of us in Isolation.

So, we were kidnapped from our barracks between 1:30 and 2:00 am. We were escorted to an Isolation cell. This was their frivolous way of trying to intimidate the so-called "leaders" of the work stoppage.

It was also Mr. Harper's way of trying to ensure that no one could reveal the fact that there was never a race riot, and there was nothing racial about what occurred.

So, we were placed in Isolation on investigation. I was later moved from Isolation in the old Isolation building to the newly completed East Building which was built to be the Maximum-Security Wing of the East Building and was still under investigation.

The South Wing was built to house inmates/convicts who were on Punitive, and I hadn't even received a disciplinary.

So, I knew I couldn't be on Punitive, yet I also knew that the Administration was losing their minds, or they had lost their minds. To put all of us on Punitive wouldn't have been a big surprise.

What was surprising and mystifying to me was how these folks had managed to categorize me as being a high-security convict. I hadn't killed anyone. I hadn't assaulted any Officers; I hadn't attempted to escape. In fact, up until 1972, I had done nothing to merit being labeled a Maximum-Security Convict.

However, I had been labeled as such, and I hadn't even turned 21 yet. So, how could I be labeled all of this when I had never done any of the high-security violations to be labeled as such?

Jerome Harper

The Commissioner, Mr. Jerome Harper, was being forced to resign by the governor because he was a con artist and not a true administrator that would organize, delegate, serve as a disciplinarian, or function as a man that took his job seriously.

So, Mr. Harper was being phased out and the Texans were being brought in.

I was called to the Warden's office where I met Mr. Pluto and Major Michael J. Eagle. They wanted to inform me that they had reviewed my jacket (files) and had failed to see anything in my files that would merit keeping me on investigation.

The tall Texan said, "No one wrote down what they were investigating, so I can't justify keeping you locked up any longer."

I said, "Sir, I don't mean any disrespect, but there were eleven of us locked up for the same thing. So, does that mean you are releasing all of us back to population?"

Mr. Eagle spoke up and said, "Son, you've got to learn to take care of yourself, to protect yourself, and to let everyone else worry about themselves, but since you were so respectable in asking your questions, the answer is yes. We are releasing all of you back into population, and I hope that you take advantage of it, do the right thing, and stay out of trouble. You all will be released this evening."

I was then escorted back to the East Building, and I relayed the information to all of the guys who were locked up with me.

I was now 18 and would soon be 19. I hadn't spent a full year free since I was 15. I had finally received a lump sum of money from an insurance policy on my mother after she was murdered that amounted to about $4,000.00, but I ended up sending almost half of the money to my sisters and brothers who were in Orange, Texas with our grandmother, aunt, and uncle.

The first purchase I made for myself was five Ebony Encyclopedias based primarily on Black History, events the media had never reported, and information that wasn't taught in public schools. I felt that all the knowledge I could get from these books would be good for me and would assist me in dealing with the predominantly white Administration from Texas that was running the Arkansas Prison System.

Even though I was still 18, I felt that my intelligence was very high and that I knew people. I felt that a new Administration had been brought in. There was still going to be a lot of racial discrimination going on and a lot of racism. I believed that reading those Ebony Encyclopedias would help me to become a lot wiser in the area of race relations. I wanted to show the Federal

Courts that racism does exist and that I'd be able to recognize any and all racism in prison. I thought I would be more equipped to communicate with these people, the Texans.

The Hoe Squads

When we were released from the East Building in Maximum Security and placed back in population, we were assigned to the Hoe Squads.

That was one of the first things that the Texans did. They changed the Long Lines into Hoe Squads. Every Hoe Squad Rider was a white man, but every Hoe Squad and Garden Squad consisted of approximately 60 to 70% black inmates and convicts and 30 to 35% white inmates and convicts.

During my first day going to work under this new system, my Rider immediately showed me and the rest of the squads where his head was (how he was thinking). He said that he was the new breed of Prison Guard. He then told us his name when he finished. I think his name was Thompson or Thomas. He was tall with black hair (he would later become a school teacher).

He said, "I know a few of you out here has been labeled as troublemakers. I'm not going to call your names because you know who you are. But you all can rest assured that I run this squad, and I run my squad as I see fit, and anybody that don't believe me will see a side of me that none of you want to see. It's a side that I won't talk about and won't have to as long as you all play by my rules and not your own."

He then picked two gougers (these are guys that are responsible for keeping the slow workers caught up and getting the grass that was left behind by the person on that row) out to work for him, and both of them were white guys.

Every day that we went to work, our rider would cuss out two or three inmates/convicts, and when we went in, the rider would put one black on the fence, write a minor disciplinary on him, or sometimes he had a black locked up.

There never was a white on the fence or a white locked up.

Racist Ass

One day I exploded and said, "Stuff like this man, I am fed up with your racist ass. You ain't tough because if you were, you would give your gun to Sgt. Norris and get off that horse so I can kick you dead in your racist, ignorant ass. I want all the blacks to quit work because you don't have no black gougers and have never wrote a minor disciplinary on no white nor has a white ever been locked up or talked bad to by you."

He said, "Willie, I'm giving you a chance to get back in line and to change your mind about the stuff you said."

I replied, "Take your *chance* shit and shove it up your ass and call the Lieutenant or somebody."

By then, Major Eagle happened to be riding by in the area, so he took his hat off, waived it, and brought Major Eagle over.

When Mr. Eagle arrived, he looked dead at me and said, "What's your problem, Willie Graves?"

I said, "I don't have a problem. Your Sergeant has a problem. He's a racist. He is constantly locking blacks up, writing us minor disciplinaries, and there's not a black gouger out here, but there are more blacks assigned to the squad than whites and both races are good solid workers, and I'm tired of it."

Mr. Eagle said, "Willie, I really hate to disappoint you, but you aren't running a damn thing in my fields and on none of my squads. I'm going to give you one direct order and if you refuse it, I'm going to lock your ass up." He then said some crazy stuff, "I Michael J. Eagle give convict Willie Graves a direct order to go to work."

I said, "Mr. Eagle, I am not going to cuss you out or be disrespectful to you because I don't really know you, and you might be a pretty decent fellow. So, I'm simply telling you that I am through working as long as he's the Rider."

Mr. Eagle got off his horse, gave his gun to our Rider, walked over, put cuffs on me, and radioed (used his walkie talkie) for a transport van to come and get me. I was taken in and put on barrack arrest (meaning I was waiting to get a disciplinary). I couldn't go to work, and I had to go to Disciplinary Court.

I was called to the Field Major's office that evening by Major Eagle and Capt. Henderson. When I got there, they told me I needed to realize that if I had a complaint about any of his Riders, I needed to come see him or his Captain.

I immediately got into my feelings and said, "Why should I have to come and see either of you about something that you both are seeing every day, and you both are choosing to ignore it, and it's hurting the blacks. The whites are alright because none of this affects them as it does us."

Mr. Eagle said that there were now white and black gougers on the squad, and that the squad would be run a lot better from then on. There was more said, and he sent me back to my barracks.

Three days later, I was on Punitive in the East Building on the South Wing.

The Punitive Grue

Once I was moved, I had the chance to really get to know Sgt. Brogan AKA *Shake a Spoon Brogan.* At my cell, he told me that if I gave him any problems out there I'd look like a scarecrow when I got off Punitive.

On Punitive, we were served Grue (left over vegetables baked in a crust) twice a day. We would receive one full meal every 4th day and six meals every 15th day. We could get two meals for three days or three meals a day for two days. It was our choice. Then, at the expiration of our meals, we were taken to the Infirmary or to the East Building Examination Room for the Infirmary, and we were given a semi-perfunctory physical to determine if we were physically able to return to Grue.

During all the time I spent on Punitive (off and on from 1969 to 1973), I never saw anyone not return to Grue. No matter how bad of shape they were in physically after they've finished their 6 meals, not one Infirmary Medical Personnel ever determined that the Grue was slowly and steadily messing any of us up physically or mentally.

Even though it was obvious that every guy in Isolation who had been on Punitive/Grue 20 days or longer had been messed up physically.

Some of us sentenced to Punitive would go the first four days without eating anything. Then, we would eat one meal, and I mean I'd eat it like I hadn't eaten in six months. Afterward, I would try to go another four, but by this time my body was so weak that I could barely walk, so I started consuming the Grue.

Since my stomach had shrunk, I started to regain a little of my strength back. Then, I just made up my mind that I was going to start eating my Grue and someone else's Grue if they didn't want it and I was strong enough to eat it.

This was how I started to sustain my strength to avoid being carried out on a stretcher like the other guys were.

Grue was like nothing I had ever seen or tasted in my life. It was a tasteless square wedge of something that carried the appearance of being cake, but it had okra, squash, carrots, cabbage, beans, green peas, potatoes, and ground beef mixed together and baked into a loaf or a square-like cake.

There was nothing nutritious, edible, or tasty about this Grue.

Guys on Punitive were losing weight at an alarming rate, but no one cared; not the Warden, Assist Warden, Major, Board of Corrections, or the East Building Security Personnel and not the Infirmary.

Guys were coming to Punitive weighing, 170, 180, 200 pounds, and losing 30, 40 to 50 pounds in a matter of 3, 4 or 5 months and looking unhealthy.

What's really important about this is the fact that none of us were given any type of physical examination or weighed when we were released from Punitive.

We had to take care of our health and get our weight back on our own.

Punishments

Being sentenced to Isolation in 68, 69, 70, 71, 72, and 73 meant that the sentence could go on for 3, 5, and 9 months or years because it was indefinite.

It all depended on who the inmate was and what he was doing.

There was an inmate named Alphonso Do or Doe Graham. He went to Isolation for not going to work. He said he wasn't coming back out until he got a job. When he went to isolation, he was weighing a robust, healthy looking 240 to 260 lbs.

He stayed on Punitive so long that we gave him the nickname *Do or Die* because he was going to do those Punitive days until he got a job, or he was going to die trying.

This man's weight dropped all the way down to 130 or 140 lbs. and he lost his mind in the process.

Those folks still did nothing to help him.

His name is in the law books on some of the different Finney cases.

The sad, inhumane fact about all of this is the Administration didn't give a damn about our health. They wanted to show us that they were not going to break or submit to any of our requests no matter how sensible and intelligent our requests might have been.

There were several guys during these years like Robert (Big Time) Williams, Alphonso (Do or Die) Graham, Percy, Alexander, Willie Montgomery, Popeye, and others whose health deteriorated really badly. Everyone saw this, but nothing was done medically.

The Warden and his staff did not attempt to put a stop to this cruel and inhumane treatment of these inmates and several more including myself.

I continued to try to understand how from ages 15-19 I was considered a Maximum-Security Convict. I hadn't killed anyone, and I hadn't escaped as a Maximum-Security Convict, which is what a convict is supposed to do to be deemed a threat to security and the good order of the institution.

All I did was file lawsuits, grievances, and write the media and politicians about the unconstitutional things going on at Cummins during this era. Yet, I was still categorized as a Maximum-Security, High-Risk Convict.

I was one of the first guys moved from old Isolation to the newly completed East Building.

The Texans were eager to establish their policies, punishments, and procedures. One of the new policies said we were not allowed to watch the white women who worked up front.

When Mr. Tall Texan called us to his office, we had to watch the Texas T.V. which meant turning around, facing the wall, leaning forward, and placing our head on the wall while leaning forward. Our heads supported all our weight in this position.

Willie Stewart

One punishment I remember vividly involved Willie Stewart. If a Hoe Squad Rider was having a problem with a certain inmate, the Rider had to call him out of the field and make the inmate stand on a milk crate for an hour or longer. The inmate couldn't move. We would also walk or trot in front of the horses being ridden by the Hoe Squad Riders, and if we were too slow, the horse's head would nudge us in the back to speed us up or to spill us onto the ground.

This was one of the contributing factors in the death of Willie Stewart. During his first day in a prison environment, they made him trot in front of the horse. Every time he slowed down, the horse would nudge him a few times until he hit the ground. When he got to the cotton field, he didn't know the first thing about picking cotton, but the Field Riders made him pick anyway. They had us taking cotton in our sacks and emptying them into his sack until Willie Stewart's sack was full. Then, they made him try to carry his sack to the end of the turn row. He took it to the cotton trailer to be weighed, but Willie Stewart didn't weigh over 150lbs. These sacks weighed more than Stewart did, and they were dead weight.

He had to carry them out of the field to the weigh in at the trailer. He had to do this twice that morning, and he fell to the ground several times. He was finally allowed to drag the sack to the end of the turn row.

The Hoe Squad Riders didn't even allow him to get a drink of water. In fact, we had to sneak him five paper cups of water on our row. When it was time to go in, Sgt. Johnson was the main one who had Stewart running (jogging) in front of his horse, and halfway to Sally Port Gate (where the Hoe Squads turn in), the Riders told Stewart to get on the trailer by himself.

When we made it to Sally Port and he got off the trailer, Stewart passed out. I don't know if it was from exhaustion, but to my knowledge, he never regained consciousness.

This is one of the times that Arkansas Department of Corrections, Cummins Unit was truly guilty of first-degree murder.

This young man was 16 or 17-years-old, and the Department of Corrections took a page out of a slave book and treated this young kid the same way plantation slave owners treated their slaves.

They murdered this youngster by ignoring the fact that he wasn't even 18; the A.D.C. Hoe Squad Riders were intent on scaring this youngster.

So, they adopted an old historical southern manner of treating human beings in a degrading barbaric manner. Slaves were made to run in front of horses. Slaves were worked until they were totally exhausted, and this is how Willie Stewart was treated. As a result, he lost his life, and he was truly murdered.

Headed Back To Prison

Around 1971, I was released and sent home.

I went home with an attitude because I was still angry about how my mother's murder investigation was conducted by the police.

I was in Hot Springs by myself because my sister and two little brothers were living in Orange, Texas with our grandmother and aunt.

I knew a lady named Lovenia Turner. She said if anything happened to my mother, she would take her kids in, so when I was released from prison in late 1971, my destination was Mrs. Lovenia's home. She hugged me, welcomed me right in, and told me to call her momma, Mother Lovenia, or just mother. She was like my Godmother, but she treated me just like I was her biological son.

I was allowed to be myself with Mrs. Lovenia, which meant my little immature, naive mind wanted me to continue to be a thorn in the police's side. I was too young to realize that I was hurting myself and not the police, so I kept on doing my criminal activities. I was committing burglaries, forging checks, shoplifting, and committing a robbery every now and then. I was graduating to using a gun to rob people. This was something I had never done before, but all I could see was a good or better chance to keep a fat bankroll and anger the police at the same time.

In November of 1971, I was 19 and has already been to prison three times.

In 1972, I made my first nice score on a robbery since I had graduated to armed robbery. My victim was a fat, semi bald, rich, white man. He was from St. Louis, Missouri in Hot Springs on vacation.

That night I met him at a bar. He came to my table, sat down without being invited, and he said, "Sir, are you from here?"

I said, "Yeah, why?"

He said, "I want to buy some black pussy tonight, and I will pay good money to the woman and you as well for providing the woman for me."

He pulled out an enormous bankroll which was full of hundred-dollar bills. He peeled off three, gave them to me, and said, "That's for you. Now, make sure you set me up with some good pussy, and you got a good tip coming."

At that point, I had made up my mind that I was going to rob him regardless.

The man had one of the biggest diamond clusters I had ever seen on his finger, a small solitaire diamond on his pinkie finger, and on his wrist, he had a diamond studded Longines watch. And a big bankroll in his pocket. He wasn't afraid to ride into the black end of town.

So, I went to the phone, called Jewell Lofton, and set it up with her. I told her she could make $400 to $500 dollars. So, she was game. I went back and told him we would have to go to Malvern Arkansas, and a street off Malvern Avenue.

I asked, "Do he know where Malvern Arkansas. is?"

He said, "Hell yeah, I used to live in Hot Springs until I left to go get rich."

So, we kept a small conversation going about money and about him being well off financially.

We made it to Grove St. where Jewell lived, and I made up my mind to get him immediately because if I didn't Jewell was going to fuck him really good, serve him a drink to knock him out, she would rob him and then put him in his car with her two male friends. All I'd get was maybe $200.

So when I got out the car to come around to him, I pulled my pistol, walked up behind, put him in a chokehold, and laid my pistol on the side of his face so he could feel it and see it.

Then, I did something dumb.

I kept my pistol beside his ear and face, pointed the barrel at a hill, and pulled the trigger. The loud noise scared him so badly that he almost fainted. I ruffled his pockets to get the bankroll and worked the ring off his fingers and the watch off his wrist.

Soon, I heard sirens, so I took him to the ground, beat him, took his pants and shoes, and started running. I ran until I made it four streets over and down to the Atmosphere Club. As soon as I got in the door, I went straight to Honey (the owner) and gave him the bankroll I took from the trick. I told Honey that half of it was his. All I wanted was for him to keep me with money on my books when I went to prison.

Honey asked me what was going on. I told him that I had done something and knew that I was going to prison for it. I just wanted Honey to keep some money for me on my books. Honey started to look worried.

I said, "Honey, none of the bills are marked. You run your business, so all your money is easily explained. All you got to do is have someone bring me $200 up to jail because this money in my pocket is going to be taken when they arrest me. So, take care of me."

The Shakedown

Then, I went across the street to the Cameo, ordered a beer, and sat down in a booth to await the police. I could see the door and anyone coming in. I knew it was $2000 or more on that bankroll, but I wasn't tripping or worried because Honey had treated me like his son since I was 13. I knew he'd take care of me. I didn't give him the ring or the watch. I didn't stash them like I was supposed to do because I was young and dumb. I felt that I could talk my way through anything.

I didn't know that Jewell had called the police on me. She had told them everything.

I was smooth as hell, I thought. To this day, I don't understand why I kept that ring and watch on.

I saw the police come through the door, and they spotted me also.

They walked over to my booth and said, "How are you doing this early morning, Mr. Graves?"

I replied, "I'm okay, but I know you didn't come to my booth for us to exchange greetings or to check on my health and welfare."

One of the officers said, "You are right Willie. We got a call on you, and we've got a robbery victim that has been attributed to you. So we need you to stand up, turn around, put your hands on the table, and spread your legs. You know the drill."

Before they approached me, I had already put one of the rings in between the cushions in the booth. They shook me down, pulled the money out of my pocket, and asked me about it. I told them most of it came from a crap game, but the rest was from working odd jobs. I was paid cash. The booth hadn't been touched yet, and they hadn't found the ring in my shoe yet. So, one of the officers saw the watch and asked for it.

He said, "Where'd did you get this Willie?"

I said, "I won it in the crap game, and I am waiting on the owner to bring me a grand to get it back."

All three officers smiled. The Sergeant told one of the officers to shake down both sides of the booth. The officer found the ring immediately.

The officer gave it to the Sergeant and the Sergeant said, "You know anything about this, Willie?"

I said, "Nope, I haven't ever seen it before."

The Sergeant said, "Cuff him, and let's go to the station."

The victim and jewelry were at the station when I arrived. The victim immediately identified his watch and the ring. He asked about his 2nd ring. The Sergeant sent one of his officers back to the Cameo to reshake down the booths.

They said, "Take him in an office and strip him."

They did, and immediately, they found the other ring. They finished the shake down because they were looking for the rest of the money. They then took me to an office where Morgan O shay, Frank Owens, and Johnny Wiser were. Morgan told me I was going back to prison for a long time.

He said, "If you had listened to me and not thrown your meager support behind Bob Griffin, I would have helped you out because the victim wants to get back to Missouri as quickly as possible. But since you wouldn't listen, you are going back into the system for a while."

He told Frank Owens and Detective Johnny Wiser to get this piece of shit out of his face.

As Lt. Oral was escorting me out he said, "Don't get comfortable Willie because you are going through the system and on your way back to prison fast as hell."

Two weeks later, I was at my preliminary hearing and refused an attorney to represent me. I was told that this was only a formality, and I'd have an attorney at my Circuit Court proceedings. With that, Judge Earl Mazzander allowed me to represent myself; then, he bound me over to the Circuit Court to go before Judge Henry M. Britt and Prosecutor Walter Wright. I think I was appointed Richard Slagle as my attorney.

At my Circuit Court hearing, I testified that the guy from Missouri was a pedophile who had come on to me, and because of that, I beat him down and robbed him out of anger. I made him appear to be a child molester.

I was convicted and sentenced to prison for 9 years anyway. I felt in my heart that my conviction would be overturned because my attorney told me it would be overturned in Municipal Court since they had failed to appoint me an attorney at my preliminary hearing.

Two days later, I was on my way back to prison.

On The Wall Again

When I arrived at Cummins, I was lined up on the wall with the rest of the new inmates.

I was standing there when a Lieutenant and a Captain came to me and said, "Let's go, the Warden wants to see you (The Warden was A.L. Tall Texan)." So, we proceeded to the Warden's office.

Asst. Warden Jerry Soup, Major Eagle, and Assist Warden Cee Bee Loren were present. All of them greeted me, and I responded in kind and greeted them.

Mr. Tall Texan said, "Willie, I called you to my office in front of these witnesses to ask you how you are going to do your time this time."

I thought about it for a minute and I said, "I didn't know I had a choice in how to do my time Sir!"

Mr. Tall Texan said, "Willie, I'm not going to play no damn games with you. I would just as soon lock your ass up in the East Building, weld the door shut, and forget about you. I can't do this because of all the popularity you've acquired from letters you've wrote to the media and the Prison Rights Groups, and your constitutional rights. So, just answer my damn questions because you know exactly what I mean."

I said, "I'm doing it in the way that gets me out of here as fast as possible."

Mr. Tall Texan said, "I don't believe you, and I'm putting you in West Hall where I can monitor your every move. I'm putting you in barracks 8 and unassigning you. You can go to yard call, church, library call, and the kitchen to eat. If I see or hear of you being in East Hall, I'm locking you down. Do you understand me?"

I said, "Yes sir!"

I was then escorted from his office back to the wall in front of the fingerprinting and picture taking room. Then, I was sent to barracks 8.

All of the guys were glad to see me back, and this was out of love. All I could think of was that I wouldn't be back in prison very long because I knew that my case would be reversed. All I had to do was wait.

In the meantime, Mr. Tall Texan, Major Dejarnette, and others wanted to do something to curtail my influence and to cause me to lose face with most or all of the inmates. I didn't know about any of this at the time. I had no idea that they had picked out a white guy who they felt could beat my ass, and they wanted this done badly. If I got whooped by a white guy, I would lose all of my influence and credibility.

So after I had been back in prison for about a month and a half, I ran across a guy named Big Time (a white guy name John Oliver). Big Time weighed about 210-220 lbs. and was kind of flabby. At that time, I weighed about 155 lbs. I was solid, and I had been fighting and wrestling all my life. So, when Big Time came to me and picked a fight in barracks 8 one night, I put something on his ass.

Jewell Boyd and Adrian Tisdale stood around to make sure that no one else got involved.

When the officers ran in to break it up, they tried to handle me a little roughly because all of them knew what was going on. They realized that it had all gone wrong as far as the outcome.

Big Time was lying on the floor bleeding from the nose and mouth. He was hurt, and I was standing over him thinking about stomping his face in because I knew why he had picked a fight with me. I was mad as hell at him for being such an ass kisser with the folks that had risked his welfare and life to pick a fight with me. I had never argued with him.

Jewell Boyd, Adrian Tisdale, and several others gathered around me and told the officer that they weren't going to treat me badly because I hadn't started anything. The officers took me to the hall desk, and the Lieutenant told them to get my property and lock me up in the East Building.

The next day, Major Dejarentte told them to let me out; they did because Dejarnette knew that everyone had figured out what had gone down in the fight incident. He knew it was going to come to light, and he could lose his job if I pursued it. He figured that if I stayed locked up I would go writing crazy.

So, I was released from the East Building and placed in barracks 12 in East Hall. I was put back in East Hall where Mr. Tall Texan didn't want me, but where I wanted to be.

The Prison Environment

In 1972, the prison environment was totally and completely evil and corrupted.

In fact, I feel that if I could have chosen the era to do my time in, it would be between 1968 and 1972. I would have chosen 1968-1970 because it was the era where only the strong survived and things like snitching and child molesting surviving in population wasn't going to happen.

When the Free World People took over in 1971 and 1972, the number of officers kept growing in population daily. The Free World Officers began to bust heads with slapjacks . The slapjacks were heavily weighted down with extra lead to ensure that they did two things: busted the inmates' heads open and draw blood. The slapjack knocked the inmate out when he was hit with a slapjack and nightstick.

More white officers were hired at Cummins in 1971 and 1972, and we black inmates felt their presences.

In 1972 and 1973, the Federal Courts tried to help the inmates out by ordering A.D.C. employees and administrators to immediately stop verbally abusing the inmates, to stop cussing, to stop using racial slurs towards inmates in any manner, and most of all to stop physically abusing inmates in any manner.

The Federal Courts made this ruling and made sure that the inmates got a copy of this ruling. However, A.D.C. employees never adhered to the ruling. They slowed it down long enough for the court to feel that they were abiding by this ruling, but they started back in 1973 and had been going strong ever since.

In 1973, I felt that Mr. Tall Texan was beginning to treat inmates and convicts like we were animals. I was trying to instigate another work stoppage. Some kind of way, it got back to the folks, and I was locked up in the East Building at the orders of Mr. Tall Texan.

So, while on the South Wing and during the time of the Rodeo, I instigated a riot while doing Punitive.

The convicts began to flood the East Wing and set cells and hallways on fire. It was smoked up and flooded with water on both sides of the South Wing. Inmates were coughing and hollering; I mean they were hollering as if they were scared and dying.

Then, an officer went into the pipe chase and turned the water off, so we couldn't flush our commodes or turn the water on. Then, two others brought two gigantic exhaust floor fans and opened the back door leading outside and to death row. The officers sent for all of the Inmate Porters to come clean up the mess we had made with the water and burned paper. When they had it all cleaned up, about one hour later, Mr. Tall Texan came to the South Wing, went to each cell, and made everybody say their names. He was writing names down.

The Rodeo was going on at the same time. Mr. Tall Texan had attended the Rodeo and was mad that he had to leave the Rodeo. He was mad as hell about the flooding and the fires. After Mr. Tall Texan visited the last cell, he stated to all of us that he was going to have the officer turn the water back on and send some of us to the Infirmary. He also said he would be talking to a few of us later on.

Around midnight, Mr. Tall Texan sent for every one of the inmates on South Wing and lined us all up on the wall in the hallway in front of the Major's office. He then walked down the line (like a Drill Sergeant) looking us in the eye.

When he got to me he said, "Did you have anything to do with this, Willie Graves?"

I just kept staring into space and said nothing.

Mr. Tall Texan then leaned down, put his mouth close to my ear, and said, "You little black son of a bitch. If I find out that you started all of this, I promise you that I'm going to personally kill your black ass."

I wanted to laugh, but I didn't because I didn't really know how mad Mr. Tall Texan was.

So, I said, "I didn't start anything, but I participated because it's hot back there. We aren't getting any cool air in our cells."

Mr. Tall Texan said, "That problem will be dealt with, and all of you have 30 more days. And I'm thinking seriously about making you live in the filth you've just created, but I won't this time."

I kept looking at Mr. Tall Texan, Mr. Eagle, and the officer's face, and I could see that they were mad enough to hurt or to kill all of us. This was the only time I could remember that I had allowed Free

World Personnel to really scare me. Even though I didn't display or show fear, it was there.

It was somewhere during this time that my case was reversed and remanded which meant that my conviction was reversed and sent back to Circuit Court to retry me. They reversed it because I didn't have an attorney at my preliminary hearing. The law stated at that time that a defendant must be represented by counsel during all phases of the trial and especially the preliminary hearing.

When I went back to the County jail, I was there for about two weeks before I was released because the victim refused to come back and testify against me. In fact, he was satisfied with getting his two rings and watch back. The money didn't bother him, but the scathing testimony I gave against him was pretty rough. He didn't want to go through it again, so I was released from jail.

This time I actually tried to get my life together and to stay out of jail/prison, but I was still young and dumb. I eventually started robbing liquor stores and grocery stores. On my last robbery, I robbed the 19th Hole Liquor Store with a guy name Kenneth Agnew.

Snitches

When we were getting away, something inside of my head said, "William, if you want to really get away scott free, you need to stop this car and shoot Agnew in the head, or you are going back to prison."

But I am not a cold blooded ruthless killer, so I ignored the voice in my head and proceeded to the house where Agnew and I went to my room and split the proceeds which was a little over $6000.

It was more than that, but we couldn't spend the rest because that money was in the form of checks and money orders. I had to destroy all of that, but Agnew and I split the $6000 dollars.

I told him to stash the money for about 4 or 5 days, and let it be held until the heat dies down.

He said, "Ok."

This was on a Friday. I went by his house that Saturday, and he and his girlfriend, Paula Stewart, had a party going on. I got out of the car and walked up to the house to check out the party and to see if this fool had gone against my instructions.

Not only had he allowed his woman to convince him to throw a party using the money he was supposed to stash, but this fool had also told Paula what we had done to get the money.

By the time I got there, everybody at the party knew what had gone down and how Agnew had gotten his money. Immediately, I began to regret that I didn't have the nerve to go ahead and shoot him in the head, so I could be done with a loose cannon.

People at the party were offering me beers and patting me on the back.

Agnew couldn't face me, so I went to him and said, "Nice job. Now let's see how long it will take for the police to get to your dumb ass."

I turned and left the party because I had seen two known snitches at that party and with his girlfriend, Paula that was three. So, I went home and packed a traveling bag. There was no doubt in my mind that Agnew would be picked up within 48 hours, and within 12 hours after that, the police would be out looking for me.

I went back to his house, called him outside, and said, "It would be to your advantage to get out of town, or these snitching ass niggas will have you in jail in 48 hours."

He said, "I'm not worried, so don't you worry."

I looked at him with disgust on my face, and I left. I knew right then that I should become a mass murderer and kill him, his old lady, and the two known snitches in the room.

But my common sense prevented me from doing something very irrational at that time, and I let it ride because I didn't want to go to prison for the rest of my life.

Orange, Texas

I went to Orange, Texas with my family.

I got a job working at Jack Tars as a waiter. I had intended to stay in Orange for a while, but I had fallen in love and was intent on getting married to a young lady named Shannon Bryant. I was talking to her on the phone twice a week every week. Finally, her voice got to me, and I foolishly left Orange to go get Shannon, to bring her back to Orange, Texas, and get married.

The day I left, I went to Lake Charles, Louisiana, caught the bus, and was on my way.

Some power was trying to tell me not to go and that it was a trap. I had pawned my car in a crap game for two thousand dollars and had 3 weeks to get it back. That's how we gambled in Orange Texas in the 80's.

Anyway, while on the bus, I met a beautiful young lady on her way back to Shreveport, LA. I struck up a conversation with her, and we had serious chemistry and connected really well. In fact, we connected so well and I impressed her so much that she asked me to come to Shreveport with her.

I declined because I was going to get Shannon, and we were going to get married. So, I turned this young lady down and proceeded on to Malvern where I was going to sneak into Hot Springs, pick up Shannon, and sneak back out of town in my sister's car.

However, when I got off the bus in Malvern, the police came out of hiding and took me into custody. Shannon had told her two friends about what she was getting ready to do and about how I was coming to pick her up and take her back to Orange, Texas so, we could get married. One of her friends notified the Hot Springs Police (there was a reward for me), and they turned me into the police by telling them that I would arrive in

Malvern on the bus and that I would be driven to Hot Springs. So, I was arrested and put in jail to wait for the Hot Springs Police to come and pick me up, and they did.

I went back to Hot Springs and was placed in the County jail. I had a preliminary hearing the following week and was bound over to Circuit Court. About 75 days later, I went before Judge Britt and Walter Wright once more, and after Agnew's wife, Paula Stewart Agnew, testified, I was convicted of Aggravated Robbery and was sentenced to 21 years in A.D.C.

I was sent to Cummins, and once again, I was asked how I was going to do my time. Mr. Tall Texan said that he had no qualms about putting me in Ad/Seg and leaving me there. So, I didn't get smart. I said that I desired to do my time and try to get out as soon as possible.

Mr. Tall Texan put me in barracks 8 again and assigned me to Pine Bluff Construction, so I wouldn't have a lot of idle time.

The Truth

Everything that was going on in prison during this time was illegal and often inhumane. In fact, a few people whom I talked to about this, felt that some of the things that were going on that I couldn't prove should just be left out.

However, I feel that by doing that, I would be withholding vital information and in essence glamorizing prison life for young people to the point where they would think that they could do the exact same thing that I did and make it.

But that's not the truth.

The truth is this: I was lucky, mentally strong, charismatic, intelligent, and I had a strong heart that was not going to allow me to be weak in *any* manner.

I was also a hell of a fighter and I didn't mind killing anyone to make life for me easier or less hectic.

This does not mean that in my young years I never had the police (Correctional Officers) jump on me. In fact, I was whipped in Disciplinary Court by Jimmy Duggan, Royce Martin, Jeremiah Robinson, and another officer. They jumped on me and whipped me with a wooden microphone holder, a telephone receiver, and a slapjack.

I was provoked by Lt. Duggan to hit him, and that was an error by me because they beat the hell out of me with makeshift weapons used at the spur of a moment.

Their intentions were to hurt me really badly until Sgt. Robinson stated, "You know he's in contact with those Prison Rights Groups and the news media, so let's don't hurt him too bad."

When they stopped beating me, they dragged me back to my cell and threw me into my cell.

I saw numerous friends beaten by various officers.

For all the violence I saw and experienced, the thing that was prevalent in the 70s in Cummins was sex.

Pickett Privacy

A lot of younger guys were made into prison wives, and it did no good for guys like me to try and save them because they didn't want to work. They liked to live that easy life in prison where they were eating good and smoking good. No one was messing with them. There was a price for the good life.

Some were raped, and some participated in sexual acts in order to get commissary, weed, and protection. Then, there were the guys who were turned into sissies from games that various convicts played with the help of officers.

Officers would write a phony, boguish (disrespectful) disciplinary on the victim, and the savior would ask the victim, "What's up young blood," or "What it is my man?"

Then, the young dude would say, "Man, I just got a damn disciplinary, and I go up for the Board in two months. I can't stand it."

The convict would proposition the youngster, and if the youngster didn't hit him or try to mess him up, the convict would keep pushing. He would even go get the disciplinary and tell the youngster that he gave the officer 30 greens for the disciplinary.

He'd give it to the youngster to tear it up himself and right then, the convict would say, "This is solely between you and me. You can ease on the Pickett later tonight or in my bed. It's your choice."

It would always be the Pickett because it offered a little privacy.

The East Building

In the East Building, the Administration contributed to numerous guys being raped or beaten down by cellmates.

In fact, I came close to being a victim myself of a beat down. I was placed in a 4-man cell with three whites, and one of the whites was dead alright with me.

I had somehow stupidly allowed myself to be tied up (my hands behind my back) because we were playing a Houdini game to see who could get out the fastest. When the tie up was complete, this white guy named Kennedy began to talk shit and strut around the cell. My partner got off the bed and untied me. I immediately began to beat the hell out of Kennedy, and my beating of him was primarily out of my fear of being vulnerable to the point that I could have been hurt badly.

It would have been my fault for being naïve enough to allow myself to be tied up like a damn fool and to do it in a cell of three whites.

I was so mad that I made Kennedy get naked and get in one of the bottom bunks. I made him act like a dog. He had to get on the floor, bark, and lick the floor like a dog. I was mad that a Punk (sissy) had fronted on me and tried to belittle me while I was tied up.

If it hadn't been for my partner, McRae, untying me, there is no telling what would have happened to me while I was tied up.

I never told anyone about this until now.

I also saw my close friend, Willie Baker, get into an altercation in the cell with St. Louis. Baker whooped him really good; then, Baker grabbed him and put St. Louis' head in the shitter (commode) trying to drown him. Cag and I had to pull Baker off of him because we didn't want any murder charges.

Then, there were three white guys in the cell with this retarded white guy. They fucked him and killed him.

The reason most of this was happening in cells was because the Administration wasn't screening anyone before they put them in a cell. They should have known that Baker, Cag, and I were best friends and three tough ass dudes also, and they should have known that St. Louis was a suspected rat, and no one liked him.

But the Prison Personnel didn't care what happened in the Ad/Seg cells or the Isolation cells.

They put Stanley Redmond in the cell with Donald Friend, and Donald Friend began to abuse Redmond because he (Friend) was bigger than Redmond. So, Friend was taking his trays.

One day they got into a fight in the cell, and Redmond got a lucky punch in and knocked Friend out. Redmond then took Friend's head and began to beat the back of Friend's head on the concrete floor until Friend was brain dead.

I was already in the hospital with Guillain Barre Syndrome when they brought Friend into the room that I was in, and I got to see him with my own eyes. Redmond had gouged both of Friend's eyes out with a metal spoon.

These are just some of the things that made surviving in prison similar to surviving in the jungle around wild animals, and it was supposed to get better when they (A.D.C. Prison Administration) began to replace Inmate Guards with Free World Guards. It really didn't get any better. It got worse.

With Inmate Guards, we knew what we were dealing with: sexual predators, sneaky killers, and guys who would extort people for sex if they were weak enough and gullible enough to go for it. A lot of young, middle age guys went for it and became prison sissies or prison wives.

When the Free World People began to take over everything, those prison sissies and prison wives tried to get their male identities back and to be men again.

In my way of thinking, that wasn't about to be possible with me. I felt that if any man had been mentally and physically weak enough to lie down or to bend over and allow another man to insert his penis into that person's rectum, that person was a sissy or a he/she for life.

I would never say anything about that person unless they tried to mislead any of my youngsters into believing that they were something else other than a person who gave up his manhood in order to live better or safer in prison.

The Lies They Tell

In 1976, while in the cotton field picking cotton, Major Sonny Henderson decided again (he was aware of Major Dejarnette sending Big Time John Oliver at me) that he was going to send someone at me to whip my ass. The purpose of these Free World Officers sending someone to whip me was first, to send a message to blacks that I wasn't tough by sending a white guy to beat me up.

Secondly, they wanted to damage my image amongst the blacks and make my credibility be almost non-existent. It was important to prison officials, at this point, to tear my image down because I was good at instigating sit-downs and riots or both.

So, Major Henderson picked this white dude that was a little bigger than me and about 5 years older to be on the row next to me. We began picking cotton, and I was ahead of him talking to another friend. Then, Major Henderson rode up behind all of us and started to talk to our Rider. They conversed for a while, and when we had gotten almost half way up the cotton rows, I heard Major Henderson call my name.

I said, "Yes sir."

He said, "Willie, I hear you have been telling people that you can whip the shit out of Carney."

I said, "Major Henderson, I don't even know what games you are playing, but I don't even know this dude, so why would I say something like that about a dude that I don't even know?"

Major Henderson said, "Willie, why would I lie on you? If you are scared to own up to what you say about people, then maybe the people around you have been giving you too much respect. It matters less to me, but several people told me you were bragging about how you could whip Carney easily.

Out of the corner of my eye I saw this white dude to my right start to take his cotton sack off, so I came out of my sack.

Seeing what the white guy to my right was doing, I said, "Man, put your sack back on. Don't let Major Henderson use you like this."

Carney stopped briefly, then, the other Rider said, "Carl Carney, are you going to just allow a black man to talk about whooping your ass and you not do shit? Don't come back to my squad this evening, and I'm letting everybody know that you are Willie Graves' punk."

With that said, the white dude rushed me. I caught him at the last minute, power slammed his ass and started beating his ass because he allowed the folks to lug him up to attack me for no reason.

The reason my rage was so severe was because I was thinking that the folks had asked him to kill me. Then, he'd be sticking me with a knife, and I would have no idea as to why I was being murdered. Therefore, I was beating his ass well, and he knew why I was doing it.

Major Henderson finally realized that the dude was not going to prevail, so he shot a shot into the air and ordered me to get off Carney.

I did so because I wasn't going to give him a reason to shoot me.

When Carney got up off the ground, Major Henderson told him to go get on his row (cotton row), and don't get off until quitting time.

He then turned to me and said, "The same thing applies to you as well Mr. Graves, and I don't want to hear no more about it."

The Cummins Era

The one thing I knew about Cummins during that era was that I could expect them to kill me if I became rambunctious or militant.

The only reason I hadn't been killed already was because I had written so many letters to the Arkansas Democrat Gazette and the Pine Bluff Commercial.

I had written a lot to Politicians as well as Gov. Winthrop Rockefeller, Gov. Pryor, and Gov. Clinton. I was writing the ACLU and other Prison Rights Organizations like the Lewisburg Prison Project, and Fortune Society in New York.

I was writing most of these places on a regular basis, so it would actually be impossible to kill me and bury my body without repercussions. The inmates and convicts would also get the word out to society if the Prison Officials should decide to kill me. However, they never decided to do this.

However, they did discuss it.

I discovered this during a fit of anger when Mr. Tall Texan, Mr. Eagle, Major Henderson, Major DeJarnette, Mr. Soup, or Mr. Dukes would blurt it out in anger.

Sometimes I believed that they were doing this on purpose in an effort to scare me. When they realized that they had erred, they would shut up for a minute. They would start talking about something else to try and confuse me, but I chose to ignore them.

You see, during this time period, I began robbing and taking other inmate's bootleg and bringing it off myself with some of my close friends. I was a master bootlegger, but sometimes I wasn't able to acquire the necessary ingredients needed to put up my own drink, so I would gather my guys together and we would take someone else's bootleg and let it cook off under our watchful eyes and protection.

Through all of this someone thought that I had got a hold to some poison bootleg because I became paralyzed and couldn't use any of my muscles. I lost my ability to breathe and had to be put on a respirator.

Common sense told me that if several guys are stealing bootleg and are drinking it together when it's ready to drink and one of us are poisoned then all of us will be poisoned, but that was not the case. None of us ever drank any poisoned bootleg. Also, if I had consumed any mercury at all, I would not be writing this book right now. I would be dead.

One day, after I had resisted going to the Infirmary, I was forced to go to the Infirmary. My tongue had swollen up, and I was losing my ability to use any of my muscles. When I got to the hall desk, (headquarters) they all thought that I was drunk and had me locked up in barracks 16. While in barracks 16, they served me a tray. I had lost so many muscles that I couldn't hold my spoon or sit up.

The Porter came to my cell and I said, "Help, I'm dying."

He ran and told the Sergeant (Sgt. Cliff Collins). Sgt. Collins came to my cell. I remembered him calling my name, and again I said, "Help, I'm dying."

He opened my cell, came in, picked me up, and took off running to the Infirmary. He never stopped until we were in the Infirmary.

My mouth was accumulating a lot of saliva, and it was to the point that the Infirmary had to keep draining my mouth. They put me on the Isolation Ward. I was right at the control center, but no one was present. I could hardly move, and I was choking on my own saliva. I was spitting and slobbering to get it out of my mouth.

Finally, about 40 or more of my friends, homeboys, and concerned convicts/inmates got into the Infirmary. They made the Nurse opened my room. Percy Alexander, Alex Boryschtsck, and Aaron Blackwell came into my room, got me out of the bed, and held me over the commode, so I could spit and keep the saliva out of my mouth as much as possible.

All the people that came to the Infirmary demanded that someone in power come to the Infirmary with a doctor because it had become obvious to everyone that the Administration intended to let me layup unattended and just die.

If these convicts/inmates hadn't come together to make Administration get me to a Free World Hospital, I would have laid up in the Infirmary and died.

Sgt. Knight and Sgt. Eldon Brown were picked to drive the ambulance to Pine Bluff.

I overheard Mr. May and the Lieutenant of the shift tell Sgt. Knight and Sgt. Brown that they could take their time getting to the hospital.

However, both of these Sergeants ignored these people and drove like wild men. When they got to the Jefferson Hospital, the emergency room people worked on me for about an hour and finally, they told Sgt. Brown and Sgt. Knight that they could do nothing for me. They said the Sergeants would have to take me to the University of Arkansas Medical Center.

The hospital workers also told the two Officers (the identified hospital officials) that they didn't have to hurry because I didn't have long to live.

But again, Sgt. Brown drove the ambulance as fast as he could with the siren blasting loudly. When we got to UAMS, I was immediately put on an artificial respirator to breathe for me because I was losing my ability to breathe. They put something in my mouth and sucked up the excessive saliva. It was like my saliva glands had burst and my mouth was overflowing with saliva.

I was given two spinal taps before they found out what was wrong with me. The diagnosis was that I had Guillen Barre Syndrome. I could have died, but through the grace of God, I survived and was pulled back from the brinks of death into the land of the living. I still was unable to walk, to brush my teeth, to feed myself, to bathe myself, or even to get myself a drink of water. A nurse had to do everything for me.

Helping Myself

I was in the UAMS Hospital and the Jefferson County Hospital for about three to four months.

Finally, after I had been on physical therapy for about two months, the head nurse came to see me and asked if I wanted to stay up there in the hospital or to go back to Cummins.

Not that I was tired of being pampered and waited on hand and foot by the nurses, but I just had a feeling that the way for me to get back to normal was to go back to the farm (Cummins) where I'd be forced to do for myself and gain back my strength.

At this time, I was still partially paralyzed in all my limbs. Even though I had been taken off the respirator and was breathing on own, I couldn't use any of my limbs in the way they were meant to be used. I couldn't wash my face, brush my teeth, comb my hair, etc. I couldn't walk or even lift 1 lb. I was totally dependent on others to help me get around.

I couldn't shower or bathe by myself, and it bothered me to be undressed daily by the nurses and not able to enjoy this type of attention. I had no feeling in my body that equaled sensation or pleasure.

I was being handled as if I were a newborn baby, and this was only serving to frustrate me because I was angry that I couldn't move my body or my limbs at all. I even needed the assistance from the nurses be turned over in bed to avoid bed sores.

Being in this type of environment wasn't truly serving a purpose to help me get better. The first thing that I forced myself to be able to do while I was still laying up in the hospital was to wipe my butt after using the bathroom.

One day a doctor came to me. He said, "Would you like to stay up here in the hospital and finish healing or would you want to go back to Cummins."

I didn't hesitate. I said, "I want to go back to the farm because The Lord showed me how I'd be healed."

So, even though I was giving up being around Free World People daily who cared about me, being able to eat Free World Foods, and watching cable

TV, I knew that I was making the right decision to request that I be sent back to the farm.

This was the one spot that was going to bring me back and get me healthy.

I was convinced that the Prison Officials had tried to kill me by leaving me in the Prison Infirmary to die; choking on my own saliva and not being able to breathe properly.

But I didn't care about that.

If I was to ever get healed, I had to go back to Cummins, get well, and heal.

Tough Love

The way I got well and healed was due to tough love from the guys.

They all did things to me that they knew would make me angry as hell. They would squeeze my ass cheeks knowing it would truly anger me, and I would try to hit them (even though I had no muscles or strength in either arm).

They would squeeze my jaws and do stuff that they knew angered me. They tried to make me try to swing at them and make me try to catch them. I tried to run or walk quickly even though I could barely stand up.

All of my true friends knew that I couldn't catch them, and they knew that I didn't have the strength to hit them with any force. But they did everything that they did to me to make me get better physically and to prevent me from getting down on myself because I was at the time an invalid.

They all knew that I could get better, but I couldn't and wouldn't get better if I got down on myself and refused to get better.

So, every day that I was back at Cummins, my friends would find ways to get in my head and make me try to use my muscles out of anger and frustration.

These guys were in prison for committing some real serious crimes like murder, aggravated robbery, and other crimes, but they banned together as one big family. They came together for one common cause, and that was to get me well and back to normal.

It took about a year, but I made my way back.

I was almost back to normal. My strength was back 75 to 80%. I could walk, feed myself, swing, run, and other things. I still had to go back to

Jefferson County for checkups and physical therapy.

None of the guys who had come together to help get me better would ever forget how the Prison Officials had attempted to murder me by ignoring how helpless I was.

And I will never forget that the inmates respecting me so much is the only reason that I'm alive today.

The Administration wanted me dead but only if they knew that they could bring about my demise without anyone being remotely aware of the fact that they had killed or murdered me.

The inmates and convicts saved my life by making the Prison Officials do their jobs to save my life. My friends forced Prison Officials to remove me from the Prison Hospital (where they could watch me die) and get me to a hospital where I could get some real medical help from a real hospital with nurses and doctors who would not allow themselves to be a part of any conspiracy to murder any inmate or let an inmate die.

I could have still been murdered in the ambulance by the drivers who were told to take their time, but these officers refuse to drive slowly to the hospital. These officers pushed the ambulance as fast as they could and had the siren blasting as well.

So, being alive today can be attributed primarily to God and the plans He has for me and to those folks who refused to be apart of a devious and evil plan.

By being alive and able to write this book, I found favor in God's eyes.

By the time I was almost back to normal, it was 1980 and I was ready to go home.

I had endured and survived the Guillien Barre Syndrome and was recovering, but in early 1980, I had surgery on my left knee for an ACL injury that I had suffered while playing slow pitch softball.

Paroled

In 1980, I had made parole on my sentence, and even though I would be on parole for a while, I still wanted to be a part of the prison. I couldn't leave prison totally free. I was released to Hot Springs Arkansas.

I actually thought that I would stay free this time because I was living with a woman whom I was crazy about. She had me going to P.T.A. meetings and high school football games. I was working at Quapaw Vo-tech as a maintenance man and I was bringing home my check and leaving half of it with my old lady. I felt like a new citizen who was supposed to be free.

I was working and taking care of a family, and I was not committing any crimes, but I wasn't going to church or any form of church functions.

So, when my rap partner (crime partner) came to me wanting to commit some crimes that we felt we wouldn't even be on the radar for getting caught over, I allowed myself to be influenced and started committing crimes again.

I kept committing crimes until I got caught and was sent back to prison. I was convicted of three Burglaries, three Aggravated Robberies, and Theft of Property. I was given three fifty-year sentences, three ten-year sentences, and one eight-year sentence. Then, the judge ran the entire sentence into one fifty-year sentence, and it was placed under Act 93 which meant that since I was a 4-time loser, I had to do my entire sentence with earned good time. At that time, I was 28 years of age and was looking at doing at least 23 years with earned good time.

The A.D.C. Compromise

When I arrived back in prison in 1982, I had to go through the Diagnostic Unit in Pine Bluff for the first time during all of my years of incarceration.

All other times I was sent straight to the Cummins Unit. I was sent straight to the Cummins Unit once again, and this really didn't surprise me any.

Once again, the Prison Officials wanted to talk to me before assigning me to a job or barracks. So, I was placed on the wall to be seen by someone, but they fooled me. They simply sent someone out there to tell me that I would be going to barracks 8 until they determined that I was ready to do my time without any chaos or confusion.

I was placed in barracks 8 once again and kept off of East Hall. East Hall was where the field workers were located. I was informed by the Warden that I would not be allowed to even remotely get out of line at that time. He said that he would have zero tolerance for anything negative in regard to me. He said that if I received even one serious disciplinary or a disciplinary that showed I was trying to manipulate his security staff, he was going to have me assigned to Administrative Segregation, and I would be there until I turned gray headed.

While I was assigned to barracks 8, my status was unassigned until the Administration could make up their minds on what job they wanted to assign me to.

This didn't mean that I would be given a job.

The Prison Officials were mentally afraid of me and what I could do with a pen and paper. They were afraid of my leadership abilities and how over 85% of the inmate population looked up to me, and they were afraid that I might use my influence in a negative way, abandon my positive demeanor, and resort back to negativity and destruction.

So, A.D.C. Officials during this era chose to compromise with me. They allowed me to stay unassigned and practically do whatever I chose to do as long as I stayed off of East Hall talking to the Hoe Squad Workers and convincing them to participate in any work stoppage, riot, or do anything negative that would cause any disruption in the Prison System.

Prison Officials

Prison Officials knew that they couldn't have me killed, maimed, or hurt in any manner because I had become too popular.

I was known at the Pine Bluff Commercial, The Arkansas Times, The Arkansas Gazette, The Arkansas Democrat, The Federal Court System, The A.C.L.U., The Lewisburg Prison Project, The N.A.A.C.P., and The Fortune Society in New York. I had told all of these people and organizations/groups that if I died in prison, it would be murder due to my rebellious, belligerent and radical attitude as well as my acts of defiance against the Prison Officials and the Administration. I explained that my death would be at the orders of the Prison Officials.

Not all of the correctional officers disliked me and my rebellious attitude. A lot of the officers encouraged me to write about the racism and unjust treatment of the inmates and officers. They knew that the inhumane treatment of inmates like whooping inmates in Isolation cells with nightsticks, brooms, or whatever they could get their hands on, needed to be addressed.

Plus, there were certain officers who worked in Isolation that would spit in certain inmates' trays on their food or pick up dirt off the floor and sprinkle it on the inmates' food. Some would rub their genitals on the inmates' bread, chicken, or hotdogs.

The officers would only do this to inmates that had given them a hard time like cussing at them, spitting on the officers, or throwing defecation on the officers. So, the officers got their revenge in any way that they saw fit.

There were also some correctional officers could be as lowdown, evil spirited, and mean to any inmate incarcerated. In fact, some of the officers were worse than any of the convicts incarcerated.

Other Correctional Officers, who were Christian oriented, didn't enjoy abusing and misusing fellow human beings who were helpless to defend themselves and didn't know what was being done to themselves. These officers wanted me to keep writing and seeking to expose the racism that existed in A.D.C.

All over the prison, there were clear displays of racism, and the inmate population was the one being affected by it the most. The black officers were experiencing this racism almost as tough as the black inmates and convicts were.

A Change Is Coming

I knew they were because the black officers were always sent ahead to do all the dirty work like break up fights or to try and quell riots or any other serious disturbance. They had to absorb any and all punishment and physical abuse that the convicts were issuing out at that time.

The white officers were being promoted faster even when they were less qualified to do the job. Even the white officers recognized what was going on, and they became angry about it because they realized that this could cause chaos and confusion amongst the officers that could get them hurt or killed.

Racism was starting to get out of hand.

The white officers began to harass and misuse the black inmates and convicts. They had the support of certain boot licking, ass kissing, black officers who condoned the mistreatment of the black inmates/convicts.

Then, there was the black officers who would harass and misuse the white inmates/convicts, and it got to be very hectic in prison.

When the inmates tried to come to society and explain what was going on, society would refuse to believe us. Society felt that we were exaggerating and refused to hear the pleas and cries for help that were coming from us.

There was so much abuse going on at this time that it almost started a riot, but we just didn't want to deal with the State Troopers again.

We kept on writing and hoping that eventually The Lord would open some hearts, ears, and eyes, and we would have our cries for help heard.

The 1980's brought about some serious changes. I had regained my health from the Guillen Barre Syndrome and although the 80's were beginning to look like the era where race relations in prison were going to get better, they didn't.

About the Author

Author William H. Graves Jr. is a social activist and motivational speaker. The author is confident that he can help turn things around in today's chaotic and often violent world by sharing his personal experiences with others.

Having made many mistakes that others are making today, Graves offers a unique perspective on change and motivation.

Uncensored, Volume I is his second book. His first book, *Uncle Willie, The Old School Angel* is now available on Amazon.

Mr. Graves currently resides in Arkansas where he plays an active role in dealing with the city's tumultuous environment.

Eiffel Tower Books

is an imprint of

The Butterfly Typeface Publishing.

Books to intelligently entertain
the discriminating reader!

Contact us for all your
publishing & writing needs!

Iris M Williams
PO Box 56193
Little Rock AR 72215

www.ingramcontent.com/pod-product-compliance
Lightning Source LLC
Chambersburg PA
CBHW052043090426
42739CB00010B/2033